MICHIGAN
ROGUES
DESPERADOS
C&UT-THROATS

A Gallery of 19th Century Miscreants

by
Tom Powers

D1531261

Thunder Bay Press

Michigan Rogues, Desperados & Cut-throats

Copyright © 2002 by Tom Powers

For information address:

Thunder Bay Press
2325 Jarco Drive
Holt, Michigan 48842

ISBN: 1-882376-86-2

First Thunder Bay Edition 2005

3 4 5 6 7 8 9 10

Manufactured in the United States of America

CONTENTS

AUTHOR'S NOTE

At heart, I wrote this book for my own guilty pleasure. From the time I was old enough to sit transfixed in a movie theatre and watch, with a handful of popcorn frozen in mid-passage between box and mouth, as masked bandits held up a stagecoach, or robbed a bank, and shot up the town as they galloped off with the loot, I've loved the West and westerns. I cut my permanent teeth on B-movie westerns, did my high school homework around Paladin and Gunsmoke, and grew to worship John Ford movies.

TV and movies led to exploring the West through books, and I became even more enamored with its frontier history and the strange, lawless, and always colorful outcasts, petty criminals, misfits, and ruthless killers that walked the streets of Deadwood, Tombstone, Dodge City, and other western towns. Then in college I was required to take — oh God save me from the bottomless pit of life-sucking boredom — Michigan history. To my utter amazement the class teased me with the barest peek at some fascinating scoundrels and a rough and lusty Michigan I'd never have imagined in my wildest dreams. I was bitten, smitten, and securely hooked. And like at a Times Square peep show, I've kept putting quarters in the slot marked Michigan's Seamier Side, and breathlessly watched the state shed its decorum ever so slowly and seductively. The hussy had me popping quarters for 30 some years.

I delighted in the discoveries that Deadwood and Dodge City had nothing on Michigan when it came to frontier lawlessness, crooks, gunmen and outcasts. The last stagecoach robbery east of the Mississippi ended in a deadly shootout in the Upper Peninsula. A master thief robbed members of the Michigan legislature after the politicos spent a night of debauchery in Detroit's finest whorehouses. A Harrison businessman introduced white slavery to the state and kidnapped girls off the streets of Saginaw to work in his bordello. Another Michigan man held the unofficial title as America's most successful train robber until he died in a hail of lead. One old coot financed his alcoholic binges by biting the heads off various amphibians and stretched the edible food envelope beyond that even attained, before or since, by French gourmands. One Michigan town became known from coast-to-coast as "Helltown U.S.A." And I'll be damned if I didn't stumble across a pirate who sailed the waters of Lake Michigan.

It must be noted that Michigan has never won the recognition it so richly deserves for nurturing such a wealth of culprits and scalawags. Throughout its history the Wolverine state produced a remarkable assortment of crooks and desperados, but Michigan's lumbering era bred outlaws, crime, and shady characters faster than Michigan swamps produce mosquitoes. I admit that many upstanding family men worked winters in the great pineries of northern Michigan. But lumber camps, from the 1860s until the end of the era in the late 1890s, attracted more than their fair share of criminals, human curiosities, and restless men. One lumber camp near Traverse City, for instance, had on its payroll an embezzler, an escaped mental patient, a former ministerial singer, and a West Point dropout.

And when these men, good or otherwise, spent the winter shacked up with a hundred other lumberjacks, they tended to seek quick release when freed, for the summer or even a weekend, from the tedium of the camp life. Towns near lumber camps catered to the lumberjacks' every whim. During the height of the lumbering era in the Saginaw Valley, Bay City and Saginaw spilled over with prostitutes, whorehouses, and saloons. In 1891 Saginaw alone boasted over 400 saloons and offered the 5,000 loggers who jammed into town on weekends almost any depravity known to man. John W. Fitzmaurice, a keen-eyed observer of the lumbering era and author of *Shanty Boy,* said of Bay City, "The horrors and atrocities nightly chronicled ... were of such an astounding nature that good men and women of Bay City were simply paralyzed, and rendered perfectly helpless to stem the torrent of wickedness."

Bay City and Saginaw had police forces, but many other lumber boomtowns went years without any form of law enforcement. And if a town had a police force, you could bet it was short-staffed and operated under a siege mentality. Kansas cow towns employed a law officer for every 200-400 citizens. The rip-roaring Colorado mining town of Leadville boasted a peace officer for every 344 inhabitants, while Saginaw had one cop for every 1,189 residents and Muskegon and Bay City averaged one lawman for every 2,000 residents. Not surprisingly, Michigan lumber towns such as Harrison, Meredith, Saginaw, Seney, and others had murder rates double that of any western boomtown.

Saginaw and Bay City had a look of permanence about them in 1870s. Fine Victorian homes lined the streets in both towns' residential areas, and downtown businesses offered the latest in suits, millinery finery, and home furnishings. Each town also had a saloon district, where the buildings looked like they were about to collapse under the weight of the sins committed within their walls. When Meredith, Harrison, Seney, and other hastily erected boomtowns sprung from the ground they were knocked together with green wood and rusty nails. The business establishments boasted false fronts and wooden sidewalks just like their western counterparts, but in Michigan, boomtowns often sprang up so fast that buildings lined streets still thick with tree stumps. If you took away the stumps and airbrushed out the forest surrounding a new Michigan lumber town, it would often look remarkably similar to a Kansas cow town or a raw-boned Arizona mining town.

After writing five travel and nature books, I wanted to wallow for a while in that seamier side of my state and investigate more fully the remarkable stories that spoke of an entirely different Michigan than most of us are familiar with. The adventures of dangerous, deadly, colorful, cruel, and sometimes just plain laughable rogues and felons who elbow their way through the following pages were written as close to the truth as my pen can get. I pieced these stories together from newspaper reports, books, and eyewitnesses who wrote of the remarkable events and people they chanced to cross.

I invite you to turn the pages and enter the world of the T. C. Cunyan, "The Man Eater from Peterborough," who got down on all fours to fight a bulldog. Or come with me and find a safe corner in the Red Keg Saloon and watch the most famous fight in the north woods as Silver Jack Driscoll and Joe Fournier damn near destroy the bar and each other in a titanic battle. Then later we can make our way to Seney and visit with Dr. Bohn during a Christmas season of which he recalled, "The most marked and constant features of the day, and nights before and after, indicated that brotherly love was absent and that peace on earth was gone and forgotten." In between all the above we'll attend hangings (both legal and illegal), the bloody culmination of a feud, and the end of the man who would be king of Presque Isle county.

I had the time of my life unearthing these stories and putting them on paper. Michigan, what a state.

ACKNOWLEDGMENTS

I am deeply indebted to two fine institutions. I spent a good many days panning for literary gold in the plentiful resources at the Library of Michigan and in the much smaller but nugget-rich Michigan Collection at the Flint Public Library. Through luck or diligent research (more of the former and less of the later) all of the remarkable characters you meet in this book I first encountered at one of those two libraries.

In many instances those two libraries contained all the information I was ever going to uncover relating to the individuals about whom I was writing. But frequently, a promising story would wink at me from the pages of a tattered local history book and then disappear like a genie back in its bottle. So, follow-up letters went out to the Peshtigo Branch Public Library and the Stephenson Public Library, both in Wisconsin and in Michigan to the Escanaba Public Library and the Gladwin County Library. Without exception, staffs at those facilities went well beyond the call of duty trying to answer questions from a person they didn't know and who lived far outside their service area. The Mason County Historical Society also proved to be a fount of valuable and colorful resource material.

Research visits to both the Saginaw Public Library and the Bay County Library System paid big dividends. And in both libraries, the staff led me to resources I would have otherwise overlooked. I was a librarian for 32 years, and I'm still amazed at the daily dedication of our public libraries and librarians.

The unsung hero of this book is editor Gary Barfknecht. He applied band aids to wounded syntax, performed reconstructive surgery on any number of paragraphs, drove me to distraction by asking pertinent questions, and helped me through a painful amputation. The book is better, much better for his involvement.

FOR BARB,

Who has to put up with an author on a daily basis.

PHOTO CREDITS:

Seney, Michigan (p. 1 & p. 126)
Courtesy State Archives of Michigan

Warren Bordwell (p. 32) and Jim and Maggie Carr (p. 96)
Wilderness Adventure Books

Reimund Holzhey (front cover and p. 38)
Bentley Historical Library, University of Michigan

ROGUES

P.K. SMALL

Ogre of Seney

You could search the skid rows of any major American city during the last decade of the 19th century and not find a more colorful gathering of characters than those who clung to the bottom rungs of Seney society. Human flotsam tended to wash up against the footings of bars and bordellos in every lumber town from Maine to Oregon, but the human wreckage that drifted into Seney, in the eastern Upper Peninsula, made it the Cooperstown for world-class drunks and bums. And the man who took the prize for being the vilest of the lot was P.K. Small.

At first glance, there appeared to be plenty of competition for claiming the honor as Seney's worst and most repulsive bum. Roaring Jimmy Gleason, Teapot Kelly, and Black Jack MacDonald had colorful names but

Seney, Michigan - 1895

couldn't lower themselves to the level of nastiness it took to become legends. Stuttering Jim Gallagher beat the snot out of anyone dumb enough to laugh at his speech impediment, and Protestant Bob McGuire grew thumbnails long enough and honed them sharp enough to use as skinning knives. Anyone lacking the good sense to avoid a fight with Protestant Bob paid in pain. Bob's thumbs were faster than a Salad Shooter and left his victims sliced and diced.

Stub Foot O'Donnell and Pump Handle Joe supported their drinking habits by working the "Seney shakedown" at the railroad station. When a greenhorn arrived by train, the boys each grabbed an ankle, upended their victim over the station platform, and shook all the change out of his pockets.

Old Light Heart's food of choice was raw liver, and his boarding room consisted of two sugar barrels turned end to end. He had lost several toes to frostbite, and when Old Light Heart slipped into an alcoholic nap, Pump Handle Joe and Frying Pan Mag invariably nailed his shoes through the conveniently empty toe area to the floor. Then, along with everybody else in the bar, they waited impatiently for their buddy to wake up and take his first step.

Standing head and shoulders below them all was P.K. Small, a triple threat when it came to repugnance. Small's eating habits would gag the proverbial maggot; the words personal hygiene and P.K. Small, until now, never appeared in the same sentence; and he was a hopeless drunkard. The Ogre of Seney arrived in the area as a lumberjack of imposing size but opted for premature retirement in order to pursue the life of a full-time drunk begging for booze in Seney saloons.

Like most of the other drunks and derelicts, Small occasionally backslid and succumbed to honest labor, but only in the most dire of circumstances. The usual work available to chronic drunks involved the cutting of roads through the forest, over which logs were dragged and which gave birth to the term "skid row." The pay stunk, but on the plus side it could be quickly converted to alcohol and poured down a thirsty throat.

But P.K. Small quickly rose to legendary status by devising a scheme that kept him out of the woods and cozied up to a regular liquor supply. He became a showman, a geek, and a gastronomic adventurer who'd eat practically anything in return for a whiskey chaser. For instance, for the promise of a drink Small would gulp down horse manure, either served fresh and still-steaming or as a tooth-busting, dried-up horse apple. John I. Bellaire — one of Seney's few honest, law-abiding, and respected businessmen and also a sober observer of the town's wildest days — said he once saw P.K. eat a live snake from the tail up for a shot of whiskey. In fact, P.K. bit the heads off so many live snakes, frogs and toads in return for drinks, he earned the nickname "Snag Jaw." A live mouse once went down his gullet in exchange for liquor, and he also picked "things" out of a spittoon and ... well, *bon appetit.*

In a sterling testament to what someone will stoop to while in an alcoholic haze, he once grabbed a pet crow out of a boy's hands, bit off the bird's head, and handed the lifeless body back to the dumbstruck kid. When he similarly bit the head off a goose at the Soo, it inspired the following childhood jingle: "P.K. Small eats them, feathers, guts, and all."

On the rare occasions when the spittoon had been recently cleaned and Small ran out of other disgusting things to eat, he'd walk into the street and pick a fight. If not too drunk, Small could handle himself in a fist fight or better yet a wrestling match, during which while besting his opponents, he would rifle their pockets for drinking money. When Small misjudged the toughness of his mark and found himself outclassed and threatened with injury, he chewed his opponent's ears. P.K. and his victims paid frequent visits to the town's physician, Dr. Bohn, who stitched their wounds.

Also, since soap and Small had never been introduced, a fight with him ranked worse than kissing the north end of a badly frightened southbound skunk. More alcohol had been poured into him than water poured over him, and courtesy of all the liquor he'd consumed, P.K. looked about halfway to complete embalmment. Contemporaries claimed that Small — both uncouth and, more importantly, unwashed — could be smelled from a half-mile away. The olfactory overload resulting from being clasped to his chest in a fight must have carried a jolt the equal of a stun gun.

And plugging your nose wouldn't have helped, because Small was hardly pleasing to the eye. Somewhere, sometime, he'd lost one fight and probably more, and his face carried the stigmata of defeat — it was dimpled with "loggers small pox," the result of being kicked or stepped on with hob-nailed boots. When the nails punctured the skin, they a left dark spot in the center of each dimpled scar. And in what can only be considered poetic justice, Snag Jaw had had his nose bitten off in a brawl. The doctor who sewed it back on bragged that he made Small look better than before the temporary amputation.

Small could usually be found with his brother Jim and another notorious drunk, Paddy Joyce. One of the great stories to come out of Seney tells of the time Paddy had worked all the bars in town and couldn't beg a drink. Growing desperate for anything to sip, he walked up to the hand pump at the public well and started pumping. He got no water because he had forgotten to prime the pump, but Paddy thought there was another reason why he wasn't getting a drink. Nearby lumberjacks heard him tell the pump, "I don't blame you for not giving me a drink, because I only want water when I'm broke."

Small and his buddies were the founding members of the Pot Hill Gang, and Small became the gang's de facto ruler. The Manistique Lumber Company had several lumber camps near Seney, the nearest on a low rise known as Pot Hill, just north of town. After all the lumber had been cut in the area immediately surrounding Seney, the lumbermen moved farther afield, and drunks, derelicts and recently out-of-work moved in. P.K. Small and friends were the first to take up residence on Pot Hill, and those who came later deferred to the camp's most outrageous and unpredictable character. During the summer when lumbering work slowed elsewhere, as many as 50 men moved into Pot Hill until fall, when employment picked up and they again moved out. Then again more than a few never cared to work again. The out-of-work and the never-going-to-work slept in the camp cabins, washed in a nearby creek, fished for trout in the Fox River, and occasionally shot a deer, all while paying court to Small.

If hunting and fishing felt too much like work, Seney made a very handy pantry. The men showed up at back doors asking for handouts from gardens and even had the brass to beg for chickens or pigs. The townspeople usually complied, because what was not given would be taken. They knew the gang cast a line for more than just fish. Baiting a hook with corn often meant landing a good-tasting, feathered trout if the fisherman lofted his line into a chicken yard. Wagons transporting supplies from town to outlying lumber camps were stopped by P.K. and gang, and offerings of sugar, flour, and other staples were requested. The lumber companies could have easily put a stop to this petty highway robbery but — probably out of sympathy for the unemployed men — never did.

Small also led a charmed life when it came to trouble with the law, that is until 1889 when he, his brother, and old buddy Paddy Joyce boarded the Seney train and robbed it at gun point. Brandishing a rusted revolver with a missing cylinder — meaning it couldn't be fired or even hold ammunition — Small and his drunken gang went from car to car robbing passengers until the trio were disarmed and thrown from the train. Seney residents treated the holdup as a joke; the law didn't. The bandits were easily identified, arrested in a saloon, and found to be in possession of some of the loot taken from the train. At his trial, Small told the judge he was so drunk at the time of robbery he had no idea what he was doing. On April 16, 1889, P.K. Small began serving a short sentence for armed robbery in the Detroit House of Corrections.

Not much is known about Small's life after he emerged from jail, but legend has it he died in a saloon brawl in Duluth, Minnesota.

JOE FOURNIER

The Man Who Left His Mark

Two authors have claimed that Joe Fournier and his exploits served as the inspiration and model for the Paul Bunyan stories. In retrospect Paul Bunyan is too tame a character to have been inspired by Fournier. The *Tasmanian Devil* — now that would be a better fit.

During the early years of the Michigan White Pine Era, Fournier blew through the Saginaw River Valley like he'd saddled a tornado and ridden in search of trouble. Born in Quebec in 1845, murdered in Bay City in 1875, Joe spent his short life at the center of the whirlwind and proved to be a man of prodigious and Herculean appetites. There wasn't a rotgut whiskey he couldn't drink, a man he wouldn't fight, a woman he could be faithful to. In the woods, Fournier built a reputation for working like an ox, and when back in his familiar haunts in Bay City, he got mean-drunk, often leaving a swath of destruction, human and otherwise, wherever he touched down. The French Canadian didn't just raise Hell; he taught it how to party.

Physically, Fournier came equipped for legends. Tall, curly-haired and sinewy, with wide, sloping shoulders and long arms, he looked super-sized. He had huge hands that could hold a double-bitted ax as delicately and employ it with as much precision as a surgeon does a scalpel. And when Joe made a fist and landed a punch on an unlucky opponent, he could knock him into next week. He had the strength of a Clydesdale, but when drinking, his temperament more closely resembled an enraged bull.

And a couple of unique physical irregularities really set Joe apart from your average lumberjack. First, if God had it to do over again, He might have shortened Fournier's neck down to where he wouldn't be mistaken for a llama from the shoulders up. And, second, topping Joe's stretch-version neck was a thicker-than-boiler-plate skull, which held a double row of teeth top and bottom.

It's one thing to be blessed with special gifts; it's another to have that innate Martha Stewart-like feel for knowing how to put one's gifts to their best and most dramatic use. When Fournier entered a saloon for the first time, he'd bite a chunk out of the establishment's solid oak bar, spit out the splinters, and announce to the suddenly hushed room, "Dat Joe Fournier — hees mark!" Fournier also liked to chew on beer mugs and spit the crushed glass at terrified tenderfeet, as witnessed and reported by Captain Stark of the Bay City Fire Department. Joe used his case-hardened skull as a battering ram against opponents during fights and even against inanimate objects that happened to tick him off. The young man was also highly athletic, especially when sober, and showed off his prowess by jumping up and jamming his caulked boots into a saloon's low ceiling and hanging there momentarily before dropping back to the floor.

The most extraordinary thing about Joe Fournier, from a perspective of more than a 100 years, is that he did not stand out as much as you'd think in Bay City, where he had a home, wife, and two children. Oh, everybody in town knew, admired, feared or disliked the big French Canadian, but in the early 1870s the area hosted a full compliment of hard-bitten lumberjacks and dangerous rowdies. The city limits enclosed 110 saloons and 80 "resorts" (whorehouses), and the local newspaper once complained that the town "has long been infested with one of the most notorious gangs of ruffians that ever cursed civilization." The river often carried dead bodies out into Saginaw Bay, saving the crime-ridden city the cost of public burial.

The bulls-eye of sin and wickedness in Bay City was 3rd and Water streets, on the east side of the 3rd Street Bridge. An unofficial tally counted 30 hotels, 37 saloons, and a pair of liquor stores crammed into two city blocks, with prostitutes over-running the entire area.

The worst of the worst was a three-story tall, block-long building known as The Catacombs, where booze and whores were served up on all floors. The building got its moniker from a basement crammed with a rabbit warren of dark apartments occupied by prostitutes. The bottom floor also featured a trap door and slide from which the luckless were launched directly into the river and often eternity. The going rate for prostitutes ranged from $5 to 50 cents, and history records that Paddy the Pig, Morphine Lou, Cup O'Tea, Kissing Jennie, Paddie the Racker, and Mag Snay worked in the two-block area but fails to note where on the above salary scale their personal services fell.

In addition to the wide variety and grades of alcohol and prostitutes, The Catacombs offered dog fights, cockfights, sex shows, prize fights, and the ever-popular rat-killing contests. Other attractions included drunken brawls that spilled out into the streets and grand and petty larceny that could be observed day and night. Police went to the area only rarely and then in great numbers.

Stewart Edward White best summed up the dangers of Bay City and The Catacombs in his novel *The Riverman,* writing, "there existed this great advantage in favour of the dive-keeper: nobody cared what happened to a riverman. You could pound him over the head with a lead pipe, or drug his drink, or choke him to insensibility, or rob him and throw him out into the street, or even drop him tidily through a trap-door into the river flowing conveniently beneath. Nobody bothered."

When not in the woods this was the world through which Joe Fournier strode, bashing heads and drinking himself insensible until he met his predictable end.

Those who worked with Joe Fournier in tall timber said he was a triple threat as a woodsman. With an ax and a crosscut saw he could lay pines on their sides faster than most. Some who saw him balancing on logs, wielding a peavey, and hopping from one bobbing log to another on flood-crested rivers during spring drives said they'd seen the like only once before — back east when they had been forced at gunpoint to go to a ballet. Fournier also became known as a pretty good timber cruiser — hardy outdoorsmen who traipsed through virgin forests searching for profitable stands, estimating their yield, and reporting their locations to lumber companies.

Ultimately though, Joe wasn't so much remembered for what he did in the woods, but for the fighting, whoring and drinking he occupied himself with in town. Those and the oddities of his skull. Though Joe kept a wife and two children in Bay City on Marquette Avenue, domesticity failed to tame him. The man chewed a wide path through Bay City's nether regions, and nearly every saloon in town sported a bar with a tooth-marked divot. Joe drank like it was a job and fought, drunk or sober. His strength, agility, reach and size made him a good brawler, and his sheer meanness, thick skull, and club-like hands made him feared. When Fournier lowered his head and rammed an opponent, he broke ribs and rearranged internal organs, and his fists sent many a man to the barroom floor for an unplanned nap. If a man was unfortunate enough to hit the floor with some fight still left in him, Fournier's spiked boots dispelled the notion quickly.

Joe fought and beat countless men within the Saginaw Valley, but it was a fight at the Red Keg Saloon that catapulted him into the ranks of the legendary. The Red Keg was one of seven saloons crowding a bend of the Tittabawassee River northwest of Saginaw. The sweeping water-etched curve served as a wintering ground where lumber companies stockpiled logs and waited for the spring floods to float them downstream to hungry sawmills. It was a natural gathering place for lumberjacks even without the saloons. One of the establishments called attention to itself by painting an empty whiskey keg red and hoisting it on a pole near the front door. The bar became so popular that the backwoods crossroads was soon known as Red Keg, which later became Averill. Inside the saloon, lumberjacks' hob-nailed boots chewed up the rough-hewn pine floors as the men cozied up to the oak bar. Any time of the day or night, 'jacks lined the bar shoulder to shoulder, and as many as a half dozen fights erupted every 24 hours. The Red Keg richly deserved to be the site of the legendary showdown between "Silver Jack" Driscoll and Joe Fournier.

Both backwoods gladiators had each fought and beaten a number of men that spring in the early 1870s (the exact date is unknown), but nothing about their meeting in the Red Keg appears prearranged. It was kismet. Fournier and Driscoll simply found themselves in the same saloon, and none of the witnesses recollected what passed between the two before the fight commenced. It just seemed that the pair materialized in the center of the room, and in a swirl of dirt and sawdust they locked horns, overturning tables and splintering chairs as the crowd backed into the corners, each spectator roaring for his favorite. Talk about cheap fun. The crowd knew instantly they were seeing the equivalent of a world championship fight and one of the greatest brawls to ever erupt in Michigan's pinery.

With a roar Fournier threw himself on Driscoll and latched onto Jack's throat with both hands as the men crashed to the floor. Joe realized he had a great advantage and began squeezing Driscoll's throat, hoping to throttle his opponent until he blacked out. Driscoll rocked and squirmed while his powerful hands and wrists managed to loosen Fournier's grasp often enough for Jack to draw desperate breaths and remain conscious. For more than half an hour, according to onlookers, Fournier tried to squeeze the fight out of Driscoll as the two struggled in the sawdust.

Then desperately wanting to bear down even harder on Driscoll's neck, Fournier put a foot on the bar rail for added leverage. When Driscoll saw or felt Joe's foot move, he brought back his caulked-boot, stomped with every ounce of foot-power he could muster, and drove the boot's hobnails into Fournier's foot. With a howl of pain Fournier loosened his grip, and Driscoll tore free from Joe's clutches. Both men struggled to their feet and warily circled each other. From choking, Fournier now turned to head butting and rushed at Driscoll like a low-flying but poorly aimed human missile. Driscoll sidestepped the rushes to the detriment of the bar, which became holed here and there by Joe's head. Finally Driscoll saw an opening, and as Fournier rushed toward him, Silver Jack drove a jackhammer blow to the Frenchman's stomach. Joe went down like a cow in a slaughterhouse.

The fight must have put Driscoll in good mood, because he didn't put the boots to Fournier. Instead Jack turned to the worse-for-wear bar, tipped back a drink, and ordered a curative double brandy for his still-gasping opponent. As long as they lived, the men lucky enough to be in the bar the day Fournier and Driscoll beat on each other would never forget or tire of telling about the fight. And because one's mere presence in the Red Keg that day conferred a degree of backwoods royalty — accompanied, of course, by free drinks for self-anointed witnesses — in none too short a time, the celebrated saloon would have had to have been the size of Joe Louis Arena to accommodate all those who claimed to have seen the fight.

Fournier was driven — literally — into an early grave in front of near-

11

ly as many witnesses as at the Red Keg, but strangely, no one claimed to have seen who killed him. In Bay City on November 11, 1875, Joe Fournier, Johnny Gorham, Joe Nichols and Blinky Robertson boarded the *Daniel Bell* on one of the steamer's regularly scheduled Sunday excursions to the picnic grounds at Bay View. The men were drunk when they boarded the boat and remained so the entire day. Arriving at Bay View, the boys "rough-housed," with Joe punching out Blinky and Nichols before reducing the picnic grounds bandstand to kindling by repeatedly running into it with his head. All men seemed in good humor on the ride back, said witnesses, except for Fournier, who raged around the boat and even bit chunks out of its railing. The *Daniel Bell* had hardly tied up at Bay City's 3rd Street dock when a still-drunk Fournier staggered ashore and into a large crowd. When asked where he was going, Joe replied, "To Hell." Fournier took barely a half dozen more steps when a figure ran up, swung a ship-carpenter's mallet at his head, and drove him into the sawdust-filled street like a tent stake. As the killer struck he yelled, "Take that you French son-of-a-bitch."

A coroner's inquest the next day quickly focused suspicion on Blinky Robertson. One eyewitness said Fournier's killer wore a bandanna, and others testified they saw Robertson running in the vicinity of the murder with a bandanna over his face. The coroner's jury also heard that at Bay View Joe Nichols claimed he could clean up the floor with Fournier, and that an intemperate Blinky and another unnamed individual encouraged Nichols, saying they'd be happy to help him. In response, Joe beat Nichols like he was a rug and then turned on Blinky. Nichols didn't return on the boat, but Blinky did, bearing the marks of Fournier's wrath. One eye was swollen shut, the other wept blood, and one-of-a-kind bite marks plainly adorned Blinky's nose.

Johnny Gorham testified that, after leaving the *Daniel Bell*, he followed Fournier and was in turn followed by Blinky, who was hefting a big maul. Gorham swore that Blinky had swung at him and missed but had struck a glancing blow on the second try, sending Gorham to the ground. Gorham said that, while still down, he saw Blinky set off in Fournier's direction but didn't see him strike Joe. Another witness, however, a bartender, testified he was talking to Fournier when a man looking like

Blinky delivered the death blow.

The coroner's inquest found Fournier died from a fracture of the skull above the left ear, and the coroner's jury charged Blinky Robertson with the killing. In covering the inquest, the local paper added that Fournier "was a noisy, quarrelsome fellow, drank considerably and in all respects was a notorious rough."

A $300 reward was posted for information leading to Blinky Robertson's arrest, and within the week Saginaw police took him into custody. The *Saginaw Daily Courier* noted that Robertson still bore the marks of Fournier's handiwork, including an "eye-lid partially paralyzed" and the other puffed. Blinky's face was multihued and looked like it had taken a terrible beating.

Robertson's trial got under way on January 24, 1876, with much of the evidence from the coroner's inquest making a curtain call. One new piece of evidence was a little ditty Fournier had taunted his companions with while at Bay View:

> "Joe was a little man
> Joe was very small
> Joe was a son of a bitch
> And the bully of them all — me, Joe Fournier."

But nobody would testify seeing Blinky bean Fournier. Many contemporaries felt that Blinky's friends somehow tipped the scales of justice in his favor, while others were of the opinion that the jury and town were thankful somebody rid their city of Fournier. A not-guilty verdict on January 27th evoked little surprise, and the *Saginaw Daily Courier* reported, "Robertson's friends left no stone unturned in their efforts in his behalf, and at the trial evidence was produced which raised a doubt in the minds of jurors. ... there are hundreds of persons in the Saginaw Valley who will go down to their graves carrying with them the settled conviction that 'Blinky' Robertson struck the blow that killed Joe Fournier."

Fournier may have passed on but he was not forgotten. In *Paul Bunyan: How a Terrible Timber Feller Became a Legend,* author D. Lawrence Rogers argues that after Fournier's death, countless stories were told of his life and exploits. Early on, the truth got stretched, and as storyteller after bunkhouse storyteller tried to top each other, the stories became modern folk tales and Fournier became Paul Bunyan. James Stevens, who penned several books of Paul Bunyan stories, said his writings were based in part on Joe Fournier and tales still circulating about the French Canadian in 1930, when the author arrived in Saginaw.

And in truth, Joe was not entirely gone even in the physical sense. His thick skull with double row of teeth was an exhibit in Blinky's trial, and the unusual cranium invited so much curiosity it remained on display at the Bay City courthouse for years.

T.C. CUNYAN

Man Eater from Peterborough

T.C. Cunyan was a performance artist a hundred years before anyone dreamed up the concept, a one-man sideshow of weirdness in a time and place where it was damned hard to shock anyone, and an endearing fool who was always good for a laugh.

Sometime in the 1870s Cunyan arrived in the Saginaw Valley to look for work in the timber yards. Short, squat and tough, he looked like a 170-pound piece of gristle. An acquaintance remembered that Cunyan also sported a short beard, was cross-eyed, and was the fiercest-looking brute he ever saw. Cunyan knew his way around a two-man saw, handled a double-edged axe with ease, and had a reputation as a good river driver.

But T.C. only worked between drinking bouts, which grew longer and periods of sobriety correspondingly shorter. When drinking, Cunyan became bellicose but harmless. He wandered the streets, staggering from bar to bar looking meaner than sin on a Saturday night and all the while yelling, "I am T.C. Cunyan, the Man Eater from Peterborough. I'm the toughest son-of-a-bitch who ever lived." The script was almost always the same, but to enhance the effect, T.C. would walk down the street while chewing on a piece of raw liver. Within minutes the blood from the meat covered his hands and, mixed with his saliva, dripped and drooled over his face, beard, and clothes. The new look combined with the old mantra made for a real traffic stopper.

Lumberjacks and the riff raff drawn to the seamier side of the Saginaw Valley's boomtowns took an instant liking to the strange apparition that materialized for a few weeks, cadged food and drinks, then moved on to the next north-woods metropolis. And as his fans learned early on, buffoonery followed the man around like a lost puppy. Once after spotting a water barrel in a Harrison saloon, Cunyan shouted, "I am T.C. Cunyan, the Man Eater from Peterborough, Half Man, Half Fish," then dove head first into the container and stuck there. Cunyan nearly drowned before several saloon regulars popped him free of the barrel. If the crowd had been laughing any harder, T.C. might have died there, up to his shoulders in water with his feet wind-milling in the air.

The Man Eater became so well known and liked that newspapers occasionally reported his comings and goings, as the *Gladwin County Record* did in 1891 when it announced that Cunyan, "although showing his age, was entertaining crowds during a visit to Meredith."

If T.C. was tolerated and even liked, that didn't mean he knew where to draw the line when drinking. He once crossed paths with a young mother wheeling her baby in a perambulator down a Saginaw street. Cunyan, while chewing on his seemingly ever-present piece of liver and bloody from head to foot, reached into the baby carriage, lifted the infant up to eye level, and exclaimed, "I will eat you; I haven't tasted human flesh for a month." Depending on the sources, the horrified mother either grabbed her baby and fled or fainted dead away. A cop arrested Cunyan, and a Saginaw judge fined him $200 for the stunt.

It was also Saginaw where the Man Eater finally had his bluff called. Cunyan was roaring drunk, bathed in blood, and scattering people into the muddy streets as he staggered down the boardwalks belting out his claim to fame. As usual, Cunyan was having the time of his life intimidating people until he came face to face with a slight, gray-haired older woman who stopped in the middle of the sidewalk and refused to budge. Cunyan bellowed his famous line. In response the lady, armored in moral rectitude, stood firm and shot a look at Cunyan that could have felled a redwood. The Man Eater tore his eyes away from the woman's fiery gaze and meekly stepped off the sidewalk into the mud until she passed.

Whenever T.C. visited Gladwin, he headed for Anderson's Saloon. He and the bar owner were good friends, and during one memorable visit Cunyan talked Anderson into letting him tend bar for the evening. Those lucky enough to be in attendance that night said the beer and whiskey flowed like Upper Tahquamenon Falls during spring runoff, primarily because Cunyan kept buying rounds for everyone in the place. When a deaf mute stepped up to the bar and signed to Cunyan that he wanted a drink, T.C. intensely watched the man for a minute then said, "Get the hell out of here; I belong to a more secret society than you do." The crowd roared, then took up a collection and presented the deaf fellow with enough money to drink the night away.

During the winter the Man Eater often made a point of walking around with his shirt unbuttoned, and on the coldest days he rubbed snow on his bare chest by the handful before punctuating the crisp air with his mantra. At any time of the year he sometimes was moved to bite chunks out of beer mugs to the delight of a saloon full of fans.

When not completely sloshed, T .C. was a better-than-average brawler who delighted crowds by besting many men in barroom scraps. He also made an enemy who took easy revenge when presented the opportunity. When Cunyan once passed out cold on a Harrison street, the old adversary happened by and couldn't pass up the chance to get in a couple of kicks plus hit T .C. over the head with a rock before friends intervened.

As he aged, Cunyan's brawling resulted in more losses than victories, and he learned to avoid fights. That is until all reason fled after a night of tipping back 40-rod whiskey and Cunyan agreed to get down on all fours and fight a bulldog. From that day forward Cunyan sported a memento of the encounter — the loss of half an ear. One source even claims that the Man Eater from Peterborough regularly made his way to the dog-fighting pits in Bay City's "Catacombs," where he went nose-to-nose with the animals. But that claim is simply too tall a tale to credit.

It appeared to all who knew him that T.C. Cunyan was on the path to an early grave, but the old rascal had one last surprise hidden up his blood-encrusted sleeve. Near the turn of the century, he turned a new leaf. Cunyan swore off alcohol and relocated to Buffalo, New York, where he moved in with his two wealthy sisters. Over his remaining years, the Man Eater from Peterborough strolled the streets of Buffalo, impeccably attired in a silk hat and Prince Albert coat.

SILVER JACK DRISCOLL

Heavyweight Champion of Tall Timber

When Silver Jack Driscoll entered a Michigan lumber town, it was damn near as exciting as a circus parading down Main Street. By all contemporary accounts, Driscoll was one of the best lumberjacks and the most feared brawler ever to break a sweat, a tree, or a man during Michigan's White Pine era. Men and boys would follow the living legend around town and in and out of saloons, hoping that either some of Jack's fame would rub off or they might be lucky enough to witness Driscoll take on a local tough in a titanic battle that, in a few years, would become the stuff of legend. As for women, at least the eyes of most followed Driscoll, and because his fame magnified his good looks, many found him irresistible. Unlike other lumberjacks, Driscoll rarely had to pay for the services of a working girl.

Silver Jack came into this world as John Driscoll in Lindsay, Ontario, in 1853. He came into Michigan as a 16-year-old in 1870, tagging along with an older brother who took up bartending in East Saginaw. Even at 16, Driscoll was an imposing figure, standing nearly 6-feet, 4-inches tall and topping the scales at over 200 pounds. Jack soon left his brother in lumber- and sin-rich East Saginaw, took a steamboat up the Tittabawassee River, and found work in a lumber camp near Red Keg, (Averill) Michigan.

Though Driscoll soon became famous for his skill at rough-and-tumble fighting, those who worked alongside the young Canadian said he was also an artist with an ax. He also quickly became an experienced river driver, plus men liked to work with and for him, and so word spread among lumber-camp operators that he was a highly regarded, all-around lumberjack. As a result, Jack worked throughout the Saginaw River watershed, the Muskegon area, and the northern Lower Peninsula, and ended his career in the western U.P. Somewhere in his journeys — no one is sure where, why or when — he acquired the moniker, "Silver Jack."

Wherever Jack worked, Jack played. Few saloons in Michigan north of Saginaw were not graced, at one time or another, by his presence, and most bar owners prayed someone would pick a fight with Driscoll in their watering hole. Oh, Jack and his challenger might disassemble some of a bar's rustic fixtures in the course of battle, but the match would near guarantee legendary status on a saloon. For years to come, men would be drawn to any establishment where Driscoll had fought whoever, and they would rehash the brawl as they levered a beer or whiskey to their lips. Even into the 1920s, old lumberjacks talked about an 1880s' fight between Silver Jack and Joe Fournier in the Red Keg Saloon (see page 7).

Driscoll was a fearsome opponent. He could twist a horseshoe with his bare hands, and his fists looked and felt like wrecking balls. And when in the mood, Jack was not above picking a fight. He'd often stroll out onto a dance floor and cut in on a couple, which almost always provoked a fight. And he never lost when sober.

Driscoll never pulled a gun or a knife but did regularly apply his teeth and feet against a rival with devastating effect. Eye gouging; the biting of noses, ears and fingers; and kicking the bejeesus out of the other guy while wearing hob-nailed boots were also all considered fair play by Driscoll and other northwoods fighters. Driscoll could be a merciless opponent, and the results were often appalling.

Though the fighting in the north woods was often vicious, it usually was accompanied by little animosity. Loggers fought for sheer pleasure and bragging rights — like the time Angus Brown invited Jack to mix it up in a bar in Evart. The two went at it with gusto and wowed the crowd with a slugfest of thunderous punches. Both men absorbed heavy damage for nearly an hour until Brown collapsed to the floor and said he'd had enough. Jack helped Brown to his feet and, exhausted, both men staggered to the bar where they eased their pain with several rounds. When they finally left, they were last seen walking unsteadily, arm-in-arm down the street.

One of Driscoll's fights even inspired a lumber-camp ballad. For all the sheer, unadulterated hell-raisin' done by Silver Jack, he retained vestiges of his Catholic upbringing and would allow no defamation of his mother's faith. The song tells of a brawl Driscoll had with Robert Waite after the latter had disparaged Christianity within Jack's hearing. The song is known variously as "The Lumberjack's Revival," "Religion in Camp," or "Silver Jack the Evangelist."

> I was on the drive in 'eighty
> Working under Silver Jack,
> Which the same is now in Jackson
> And ain't soon expected back.
>
> There was a chump among us
> By the name of Robert Waite,
> Kind of slick and cute and tonguey,
> Guess he was a graduate.
>
> He could gab on any subject
> From the Bible down to Hoyle,
> And his words flowed out so easy,
> Just as smooth and slick as oil.
>
> He was what they called a skeptic,
> An he loved to sit and weave
> Highfalutin' stories
> Telling what he didn't believe.
>
> One day while we were waitin'
> For the flood to clear the ground,
> We all sat smoking cheap tobacco
> And hearing Bob expound.
>
> "Hell," he said, "is all a humbug."
> And he showed as clear as day
> That the Bible was a fable,
> And we 'lowed it looked that way.
>
> Miracles and suchlike
> Was too thin for him to stand;
> And for Him they called the Savior,

Why, he's just a common man.

"You're a liar!" someone shouted,
"And you got to take it back!"
Then everybody started:
'Twas the voice of Silver Jack.

He chucked his fists together,
And he shucked his coat and cried,
" 'Twas by that there religion
That my mother lived and died.

"And although I ain't always
Used the Lord exactly right,
When I hear a chump abuse him,
He must eat his words or fight."

Now this Bob weren't no coward,
And he answered bold and free,
"Stack your duds and cut your capers,
For there ain't no flies on me."

They fought for forty minutes,
And the lads would hoot and cheer
When Jack spit out a tooth or two
Or Bobby lost an ear.

But Jack kept on reasonin' with him
Till the cuss begin to yell,
And Bob 'lowed he'd been mistaken
In his views concerning Hell.

Then Jack he got Bob under
And he slugged him onc't or twic't,
And Bob straightway acknowledged
The divinity of Christ.

So the fierce discussion ended,
And they got up from the ground,
An' someone fetched a bottle out

And kindly passed it around.

And they drank to Jack's religion
In a quiet sort of way,
And the spread of infidelity
Was checked in camp that day.

Jack was a skilled lumberjack, but it was his prowess at eye gouging, ear chewing, tooth extraction, and reducing strong men to whipped curs that moved him to the top of the list of job candidates with several lumber companies. He took a position as "head ass-kicker" with a timber company on the Muskegon River that found itself slowly going broke because a competing firm had hired a vicious thug as their lead river driver. The bully controlled the river and pulped anyone other than his own crew who drove logs downstream to the mills. Silver Jack and the bully soon met and fought to a bloody, exhausted draw, but Driscoll's employer never again had any trouble gaining fair access to the river.

News traveled fast. When another company began losing money because of the strong-armed tactics of a rival firm's paid enforcer, Driscoll was hired to set matters straight. After an hour's fight, Silver Jack whupped the other company's river shark by laying him out with an upper cut. The beaten man rose from the floor with his hand out and said, "I want to shake hands with you; I believe we can work together."

Although Jack was well liked by many, he also compiled a long list of enemies. You can't wade through the state, besting and often embarrassing loud-mouthed, two-fisted tough guys and not leave a thirst for revenge in your wake.

And Silver Jack had another enemy he could never turn his back on — booze. When not in the pinery, Jack lived in Saginaw and Bay City saloons, renting bar space by the glass, swilling rotgut whiskey like he was on a one-man mission to drink Michigan dry. Many nights Jack's bed ended up being whatever alley he was thrown into or staggered down before passing out.

Driscoll also served two stretches in Jackson State Prison, and both were attributable to alcohol. On February 26, 1873, he began serving his first term, for robbery. An old friend, having seen Jack on the down and outs (Driscoll had probably drunk himself penniless), offered to share his room for the night. The "good friend" awoke the next morning to find that his watch, some money, and Driscoll had disappeared. While Driscoll was undoubtedly in the nearest bar wetting down a painful hangover, his friend went to the police and swore out a warrant. Given the evidence, the prosecution could have sent "Babe," Paul Bunyan's Blue Ox, to try the case and gotten a conviction. Driscoll walked out of Jackson State Prison on May 5, 1877, but stayed clear of the law for only three years.

In July 1880, after Driscoll had slipped into an alcoholic stupor in a Saginaw bar, someone salted his pockets with $2.50 and a revolver, then went to the police claiming a drunken Driscoll had robbed him of $2.50 at gunpoint. The Saginaw police didn't have far to look before discovering Driscoll passed out in a saloon in possession of exactly $2.50 and a pistol bulging another pocket. The police immediately dragged him off to jail, and Driscoll awoke in a cell the next morning, with no memory of the previous night.

Justice proved swift, though misguided, and within days Jack faced a guilty verdict. When asked if he had anything to say before the judge pronounced sentencing, Driscoll, as quoted in the *Saginaw Morning Herald,* replied, "Yes, your honor; I have not had a fair trial. When my most important witnesses were testifying, some of the jurymen were asleep, and others were getting drinking water and paid no attention to what was being said." Jack again proclaimed his innocence* and spoke as if he expected a new trial.

When the judge handed down the severe sentence of 15 years at hard labor, Jack "exhibited no particular emotion, but those who could read his moods could see that the sentence was greater than he expected, and that he accepted it in ill grace," reported the *Herald*. The paper also proved to be clairvoyant, having predicted days earlier that the "notorious character will get his just deserts" and hoped the trial would be the first step in rid-

---

*Some sources say the pistol planting was just a friendly practical joke, but since no one came forth to set the record straight, even after his conviction, it's much easier to believe claims that enemies bought him enough drinks to put him under the table, then framed him.)

ding the city of "a disreputable gang who have been pestering this community for years."

Throughout the trial, officials fretted over the possibility of someone trying to spring Driscoll from either the jail or the courthouse. By the time Jack was sentenced, official paranoia had risen to the point that the sheriff placed a heavy guard around the prisoner then, while "hard labor" still reverberated in the courtroom, rushed him from the courthouse through a large crowd and threw him aboard a waiting train. The Saginaw paper claimed that "twenty minutes after sentencing (Driscoll) was whirled away on cars to his old home."

Silver Jack did not adapt well to prison and frequently was in or around trouble. In one instance, a quarrel between Jack and his three cellmates erupted into a full-blown fight, during which one of the trio pulled a knife and stabbed Driscoll several times. He luckily escaped serious injury, and later nearly escaped from prison. Jack, who worked in the prison shoe factory, had two friends pack him in a large crate of shoes and nail it shut. An alert guard became suspicious and foiled the escape when he discovered one of the crates weighed considerably more than the others.

The *Saginaw Morning Herald* and many of its readers may have been happy to see the last of Silver Jack Driscoll, but many friends believed he was the victim of justice rather than a victimizer of society. While Driscoll tried to break out of Jackson, others worked at getting him released legally. Both John McIsaac, a Saginaw cop, and State Senator John Schuch, also of Saginaw, maintained Driscoll was framed while drunk. The evidence and influence of friends led to Governor Luce pardoning Driscoll on October 25, 1889.

Free after serving nine years for a crime that hadn't been committed, Driscoll headed north to the U. P., where Danny Dunn hired him as a barkeep at his Seney saloon. There, Jack kept things under control, more from the respect he was accorded for his reputation as a feared brawler than by actually fighting. In fact, when he discovered that Dunn planned to sic him on rival saloon and bordello owners, Jack, rather than fight, quit and headed farther west. He turned up as a bartender in Duluth, Minnesota, and later as a foreman overseeing the surfacing of Superior, Wisconsin's streets with cedar blocks.

Silver Jack finally returned to his first calling, felling trees and riding them downriver. He took up semipermanent residence in L'Anse, at the eastern base of the Keweenaw Peninsula, and worked in lumber mills around the Yellow Dog River farther east near the Huron Mountains.

Another of the enduring myths adding to the legend of Silver Jack revolves around his supposed secret discovery of gold and silver mines. Folks in L'Anse said Jack regularly headed off into the wild, rugged Huron Mountains, then after a week or two popped back into town totin' a bag of gold and silver. Townsfolk and strangers alike would ply Driscoll with drink, attempting to float the location of the mines out of him. When booze proved ineffectual, others tried but failed to follow Jack when he headed back into the wilderness, supposedly to his gold and silver cache.

The thought of Silver Jack discovering and working gold and silver mines seems preposterous for several reasons: Jack had no previous mining or prospecting experience, he never flashed any of his fortune around L'Anse, and in spite of his "riches," he continued to work as a lumberjack and cadge free drinks. More likely, Driscoll loved playing practical jokes, and the idea of his birthing the rumor to put one over on the citizens of L'Anse doesn't seem at all farfetched. Driscoll would have gotten a huge kick out of bamboozling the entire town, plus all the free alcohol poured his way must have been his idea of heaven.

Yes, Silver Jack thought highly of practical jokes and might have even died laughing if he had known that his end came as the unwitting butt of his own carefully planned prank.

The winter of 1894-95 still found Driscoll working for the L'Anse Lumber Company on the Yellow Dog River. While preparing for the spring drive he fell into the river and, depending on the source, contracted a bad cold, developed pneumonia, or suffered from an attack of "la grippe." Whichever, Silver Jack went to L'Anse to recover, staying in the Ottawa House, a popular lumberman's hotel. He had been there two full weeks and felt near well enough to return to work when the calendar rolled around to March 31st.

Now a bona fide, sanctified, and universally recognized practical joker can't let April Fools day pass without fooling somebody. Tain't right. So on the evening of March 31, Driscoll took Mrs. Belanger, the hotel owner's wife, aside and asked her to help play a practical joke on Oliver, the hotel's handyman and Driscoll's friend. Jack asked Mrs. Belanger to walk into his room the next morning and shout out her discovery that Driscoll had died during the night. At the news, Jack was sure that Oliver would run into his room, and when he did, Driscoll would sit up and yell, "April Fools."

The next morning as planned, Mrs. Belanger entered Driscoll's room and announced to all that Silver Jack was dead. Trouble was, he really *was* dead and, said Mrs. Belanger, wouldn't be doing any rising up until judgment day. The coroner arrived later and authenticated the death, but attributed no cause. Whether Driscoll succumbed to his illness or suffered a heart attack, stroke, or aneurysm is not known. Under Silver Jack's pillow the coroner found a bottle of cough medicine, a Bowie knife, and $85 with a note reading, "This will be enough to bury me." A grief-stricken Oliver refused to enter the room of his good friend.

Following a funeral attended by his many friends, Silver Jack Driscoll was buried in an unmarked grave in the Catholic cemetery in L'Anse.

Though Silver Jack's life ended, his legend had just begun. He would be talked about, sung about, and argued about for decades. Old lumberjacks never tired of telling of the time they saw Silver Jack fight a local tough or even that they just propped an elbow on the same bar as Driscoll. And not a few espoused the opinion that Driscoll was a damned bully who never fought fair, often picked on the defenseless, and seldom refrained from putting the boots to his opponent. And it hardly needed pointing out that he was a hopeless drunk and a thief.

There's no doubt the man had a terrible weakness for alcohol, and it brought him grief and even jail time. But those who knew Driscoll well or spent time with him when he was sober talk of a completely different individual. John Bellaire, a respected and careful contemporary observer of the lumbering era, for instance described Driscoll as "rugged, lovable, a friend of the weak" and remembered him as a formidable charmer of women. John Fitzmaurice also knew the life of lumberjacks intimately. He moved from camp to camp selling them hospital insurance, and his book *Shanty Boy* provides a remarkably vivid description of life in the north woods. In his writings Fitzmaurice tells of a 15-mile tramp he once had to make from West Branch to the AuGres River, during which he was surprised to find himself accompanied by the notorious Silver Jack Driscoll. The author was hesitant at first, but by the end of the jaunt he admits that he found Driscoll to be great company, and the 15 miles proved to be one of the most memorable trips of his life.

At his core, Silver Jack Driscoll was a lot like a bolt of lightening — wild, elemental, unpredictable, awe-inspiring and dangerous, and the closer you got, the more unforgettable the experience.

WARREN BORDWELL

Opera Pimp

Saginaw during the 1870s and '80s was the penultimate good-time party town for lumberjacks from throughout the valley of the same name. And in the later years of that era, when railroads reached into the tall timber, shanty boys from across the state boarded trains on Friday and headed for a weekend of hell-raising in the town. The partying began before trains left their stations, and by the time they neared Saginaw, a whistle would have been superfluous, since after a few weeks in the woods it didn't take much alcohol to transform hormonal overload into an ear-splitting, primal howl. And hell, lumberjacks also simply loved to caterwaul and roar for the sheer pleasure of it, and bad whiskey proved a better lubricant than WD-40 when it came to strained or rusty vocal chords.

The carnal, whiskey-soaked noise emitted by a trainload of liquored-up lumberjacks rattled windows, frightened children, spooked horses, and caused saloonkeepers and prostitutes to salivate like Pavlovian dogs. Saginaw often hosted 5,000 loggers on a typical weekend, and the city welcomed every last drunken sot with open arms.

Well-intentioned people said lumberjacks acted the way they did because there weren't any alternatives. So periodically, reformers opened Christian reading rooms and temperance hotels. They all failed miserably.

When lumberjacks hit town they specifically wanted what came in barrels, bottles or corsets, and hundreds of saloons, bawdy houses, and freelance prostitutes served the lumberjack trade. Belle Stevens ran the city's most-refined, high-toned bawdyhouse, and her high prices kept the common element from darkening the door or messing up the sheets. While Belle didn't cater to the logger trade, plenty of other madams stepped in to fill the demand including Ma Smith, Emma Keys, Long Minn, and Carrie Lee. The vilest of the saloons and whorehouses even hired runners, who met the testosterone- and booze-fueled loggers at the Potter Street Train Station and led the drunkest of the bunch back to the worst of the dives.

In the midst of the depravity stood an apparent cultural oasis, an Opera House owned by Warren Bordwell. However, the only arias heard inside were, "Aria thirsty honey?" or, "Hey handsome, aria lookin' for a good time?" for Bordwell's was an opera house in name only. In reality it was counted among the city's better class of whorehouses, ranking just below Belle Stevens' establishment as a class place to watch a floor show, have a drink, and buy a few minutes of intimate attention from a young woman.

Bordwell's choice of name was a shrewd business maneuver. So what if the inside of his establishment looked like any other large show bar, the name Opera House reeked with class. Men who came here to drink and frolic with "fallen women" felt as if they weren't bedding common whores — that happened in a whorehouse. "Bordwell's Opera House" spoke of sophistication, talented and beautiful women, and refined tastes. Hell, slipping under the covers with a knowledgeable and willing woman at Bordwell's Opera House even held the promise of a culturally uplifting experience.

Bordwell's stood on the corner of Jane and Washington streets. The main saloon featured a sawdust-covered floor, an oak bar paralleling one wall, and tables and chairs facing a raised stage at the far end of the room. Occasionally Bordwell did book a legitimate act, but most of the time, house prostitutes danced the can-can or moved provocatively to whatever tune a small house band played. The girls also got a percentage of every drink they could talk a customer into buying, with the biggest profits coming from a house wine, sold by the bottle, that was so bad that instead of a bouquet it wielded a club.

Between flouncing about on stage and selling drinks, the girls took customers into two large "Wine Rooms," where they dispensed ministrations in 10 to 12 smaller, private tasting rooms that lined the walls. Bordwell expected his girls to move the booze and maintain a steady parade to the little rooms set aside for sex.

Bordwell also encouraged the town's freelance prostitutes to bring their johns with them to the Opera House or simply come visit and romance his saloon's customers. Though barred from the Wine Rooms, the self-employed hookers could rent a couple of "guest" bedrooms on the second floor for a buck a trick, with each room often earning Bordwell $20 to $30 a night.

The Opera House's specialty was under-age prostitutes. Bordwell lusted after teen and pre-teen girls and reputedly took great personal interest in introducing each to a life of prostitution and personal debasement.

He took special interest in Frankie Howe, who turned up in Saginaw in the early 1870s in search of her married sister and a home after her mother had died and her father had deserted her. But before the 14-year-old found her sibling, Warren Bordwell found her. He offered the penniless waif jobs as a dancer in the saloon and drink hostess in a Wine Room, but forbid the virgin to follow any man into one of the "tasting rooms."

Over the course of the next few days, Bordwell introduced Frankie to alcohol and then one night, after getting her drunk, raped her. Warren promised to marry Frankie, but instead she became wedded to alcohol and remained Bordwell's off-and-on mistress and plaything for the rest of his life, during which time she underwent three abortions on orders from her keeper.

Warren Bordwell also evidently subscribed to the lie that, "clothes make the man." As if to disguise the fact he dealt in human misery, he almost always dressed to the "nines" — often in a dark tux set off by a white shirt with French cuffs, gold watch chain stretching across a dark vest, a handkerchief poking out of the tux's breast pocket, and with a pair of gray dress pants completing the ensemble. Bordwell also sported a light mustache and slicked back his hair. And the whoremaster/pedophile's pleasant face could have been mistaken for a preacher's, except for his dark, hard eyes that appeared cold and empty.

The well-dressed, good-looking, successful bar and bordello owner was also a petty thief who made plenty of chump change. That is, whenever he worked behind his bar he regularly shortchanged both drunk and sober customers with equal success. Also, Bordwell "hired" a half dozen muscular, surly bouncers, whose only pay to maintain order in the saloon and Wine Rooms came from rolling drunks and rifling the pockets of anyone their boss ordered thrown out of the club.

In 1892 Saginaw passed an ordinance requiring establishments that held shows or theatrical performances to obtain a license. Bordwell paid no attention to the ordinance and never got a license, and as a result, to his surprise, was arrested in December 1895. A judge imposed a $100 fine,

Warren Bordwell

which Bordwell thought about appealing but paid.

Three years later Warren Bordwell died, leaving an estate worth the then-significant sum of $15,000. While nieces and nephews were identified, counted, and added to the list of people expecting to get a piece of the estate, Frankie Howe wasted away in the Saginaw County Poorhouse.

Within a few short years, the last of the lumberjacks moved from the Saginaw Valley to timberlands in the U.P. and even Oregon and Washington state. Madams and hookers followed their customers, and saloons and bordellos closed, laying dusty and deserted until they were torn down and a new Saginaw rose in their place.

It's almost as if Bordwell foresaw the end of the lumbering era and left early to claim a choice spot in Hell.

DESPERADOS

REIMUND HOLZHEY

Jesse James of the North Woods

When German immigrant Reimund Holzhey stepped from the woods brandishing a six-shooter in each hand and held up a stagecoach in Gogebic County on August 25, 1889, he was fulfilling a life-long dream. He also happened to be committing the last stagecoach robbery in Michigan and the last east of the Mississippi.

By the 1880s the Upper Peninsula had become more than just a vast timber yard for lumbermen and lucrative money pit for copper- and iron-mining companies. The peninsula's sparkling lakes and pristine wilderness were also playgrounds and vacation spots for the rich. The U.P.'s largest inland lake, Gogebic, especially lured wealthy Wisconsin and Illinois fishermen, who came for the rustic charm, the cool summer breezes, and to wet a hook in one of the greatest smallmouth and largemouth bass fisheries in the Midwest.

The Milwaukee, Lake Shore and Western Railroad led the charge to the Lake Gogebic area. The company built the White House Inn on the lake's southern shore then trumpeted the wonders of Lake Gogebic to the wealthy in the Industrial Belt to the south. The railroad delivered vacationers bound for the White House Inn to Gogebic Station, where they boarded a stagecoach (also operated by the railroad) for a scenic, 10-mile ride to the inn.

The new tourist industry expanded the job market in the U.P. In addition to lumbering and mining, men found work as hunting and fishing guides for the wealthy. After drifting through lumber camps in both the Upper Peninsula and northern Wisconsin, Reimund Holzhey, too, worked as a fishing guide before leaving the north woods and roaming the west.

The tug pulling him westward may well have been his infatuation with Jesse James. From Reimund's first days in America he hero-worshiped the Missouri outlaw. U.P. friends remember the young immigrant loved to pretend he was Jesse James. He'd hide behind a tree, fill each hand with a revolver, then leap from his hiding place and announce in broken English, "This is a stick up." Reimund honed his Jesse James impersonation by once robbing an Indian at gunpoint. When the impoverished victim emptied his pockets of his last three cents, the embarrassed would-be thief returned the coins.

The trip west, on the other hand, evidently emboldened the Jesse James wannabe, because on his return, Holzhey embarked on a spree of train and stagecoach robberies throughout northern Wisconsin during the spring and summer of 1889. Carrying a sack and a revolver, the highwayman's *modus operandi* was to enter a railroad coach and work his way down the aisle asking each and every passenger for a donation. The robberies were bloodless, but that was about to change.

Probably to escape the heat of a Wisconsin manhunt for him, Holzhey drifted into the U.P. in late summer 1889 and resumed work as a fishing guide in the Lake Gogebic area. One of his customers was Adolph Fleischbein, an Illinois banker who Reimund mistakenly concluded carried a fat bankroll. When Holzhey heard that Fleischbein would be on the White Inn stage with a number of other well-heeled sportsmen, the opportunity for easy pickings was too much to pass up — Jesse James would steal again.

As the White Inn stage made its way over the highlands between Lake Gogebic and the railroad station on what has ever since been known as "Holzhey's Hill," the gunman stepped out from behind a tree, leveled two handguns at the stage, and shouted, "I'm collectin'. Donate."

As Fleischbein and other occupants of the stage stared in disbelief, businessman Donald MacArthur slipped a hand into his pocket, pulled out a derringer, and said, "Here's mine," as he pulled the trigger. MacArthur missed, but the sharp bark of the pocket gun acted like a tripwire attached to the outlaw's guns. The highwayman let loose a fusillade of lead, emptying both pistols into the stagecoach. MacArthur took a bullet in the roof of his mouth, another tore into his leg, and Fleischbein was hit twice in the stomach. The tumult spooked the horses, which, out of the driver's control, tore off down the road from a dead start, throwing the wounded banker from the coach.

With the stage receding behind a cloud of dust, the shooter walked over to where Fleischbein lay bleeding in the road, rifled the stricken banker's pockets, and disappeared into the woods. Holzhey's take amounted to a $10 gold piece, a $5 bill, a pocketbook, and a gold watch and chain. Fleischbein lay in the dirt for two hours before help arrived. He was carried to the hospital in Bessemer where he died the next morning. MacArthur survived his wounds.

The stickup caused a sensation. The Milwaukee, Lake Shore & Western R. R. posted a $1,000 reward, plus two Wisconsin railroads — suspecting Holzhey was the same man who'd robbed them earlier in the year — each posted additional $1,000 rewards. Belleville, Illinois, Fleischbein's hometown, and Gogebic County also offered rewards, bringing the pot to nearly $5,000. Every lawman in the western U.P. and northern Wisconsin kept a sharp eye out for a man described as 5-feet, 7-inches tall, weighing 160 pounds, and who had a wart or scar under his right eye, a drooping mustache, and a set of ears that would make it difficult to walk against the wind.

Anxious to end the manhunt, the railroads also hired the Pinkerton Detective Agency. The Pinkertons descended upon Shawano, Wisconsin, after hearing Holzhey had been seen there. Another hot lead sent the detectives to Holt, Wisconsin, when whispers reached certain ears that the killer had stayed with a village family during the Wisconsin train robberies and also used the time to court their daughter.

All the leads, however, turned colder than a Pellston winter and for good reason. Holzhey hadn't gone anywhere. He had hidden in the woods for two days near the scene of the shooting, living off what few berries and fruits he could gather, and then hopped an east-bound train.

The fugitive rode the rails for almost 100 miles before jumping off in the sleepy little mining village of Republic. Hungry and tired, Holzhey had the bad luck to take a room in a hotel owned by William O'Brien, a retired Marquette police officer. O'Brien registered the stranger, who called himself Henry Plant, then spent several ill-at-ease hours while his subconscious tried to percolate something into a conscious thought. There was something oddly familiar and troubling about the stranger's looks, and the ex-lawman finally latched on to what. O'Brien rifled his office to locate the *Marquette Mining Journal* issue about the Gogebic stage robbery. When he reread the story and the stickup artist's description, O'Brien was convinced he'd just rented the killer a room in his hotel.

The ex-cop sent word of his suspicion to both the county sheriff and the town marshal. Wanting a good look at the suspect, both lawmen pocketed their badges and ate their evening meal, along with a clueless but very hungry stagecoach robber, in the hotel dinning room. The lawmen agreed the man was probably the killer and along with O'Brien they took turns watching Holzhey's hotel room throughout the night.

Immediately after Reimund left the hotel the next morning, the two lawmen wrestled him to the ground and informed him he was under arrest, whereupon the killer turned into a 160-pound wildcat, testing the mettle of both lawmen. When Holzhey attempted to draw a gun, a nightstick to his head took all the fight out of him. At the time of his arrest, Holzhey carried two handguns, a knife with a 12-inch blade, and Fleischbein's pocketbook, watch and chain.

Holzhey was transported to the county jail in Marquette, where he confessed to the holdup, two train robberies in Wisconsin, and no small amount of humiliation for being arrested in a two-bit town

For this "mugshot," taken at the Bessemer jail, Holzhey's captors dressed him up to look the part of a dangerous highwayman.

like Republic. He was then taken to Bessemer, where he stood trial and was convicted of armed robbery and first-degree murder. On November 16, 1889, Holzhey was sentenced to double life at the nearly brand-new penitentiary at Marquette.

The Jesse James wannabe became Prisoner 37 and hadn't served six months when he got the chance to kill again. On the evening of March 6, 1890, Deputy Warden Hawley asked Corrections Officer Palliser to bring Holzhey to his office. Prisoner 37 had been acting strangely all day, and the deputy warden wanted to know why. Palliser unlocked Holzhey's cell door, had him step out into the hall, then turned his back on the convict to relock the cell door. In an instant Palliser's life expectancy looked shorter than that of a chicken's at a Tyson packaging plant. Holzhey grabbed the guard from behind, held a shiv to his neck and, while in that deadly embrace, walked Palliser to the prison rotunda. In full view of the guard post that overlooked the rotunda, Holzhey announced that a correctional officer better kill him before he killed his hostage.

When Deputy Warden Hawley arrived at the scene, the prisoner was still using Palliser as a human shield and taunting the other guards. Seeing the deputy warden armed with a rifle, Holzhey pushed his hostage away, exposed his own body for a bare second, then pulled his human shield back in place before Hawley had a chance to shoot. This cat-and-mouse game went on for some time until Palliser added his own weight to the momentum of the push, broke free, and ran down a hallway with the angry, knife-wielding convict in pursuit. Palliser made it to a door and safety, but Holzhey wasn't finished yet. He grabbed another inmate, Meservey, as a hostage and threatened to kill him.

Warden Tompkins, who had been away from the prison, returned to find Prisoner 37 holding a knife to Meservey's neck. The warden grabbed a rifle and, looking for a clear shot, silently stalked Holzhey from the upper gallery of the rotunda.

Growing tired from standing on his feet and manhandling a hostage, Holzhey led Meservey to a bench. When the pair sat down, Holzhey momentarily pulled the knife away from his captive's throat. With the skill and coolness of a highly trained SWAT marksman, Tompkins shot the knife, a thumb and two fingers from Prisoner 37's hand.

After the wound had healed, Holzhey stood trial again and was sentenced to solitary confinement, which outraged Prisoner 37, who claimed he was being unfairly treated. After all, wasn't a mangled hand punishment enough? As a protest, Holzhey refused to eat or talk. The warden became so concerned over the inmate's health and loss of weight, that he wrote informing the governor he would have Prisoner 37 force-fed unless there was a change in behavior.

From then until his parole in 1914 there's only one brief notation in Holzhey's prison record, and it's a puzzler. On November 20, 1893, three years after the hostage incident, Holzhey was temporarily and inexplicably transferred to the Ionia Asylum for eight months. Why? One writer has hinted that Holzhey may have undergone a frontal lobotomy, but that drastic procedure cannot be confirmed.

After release from prison Holzhey worked in Marquette, then hired on as an occasional guide at the ultra-exclusive Huron Mountain Club, which is especially surprising since the club's owner-members were some of the Midwest's richest people. You would think a millionaire might feel somewhat uncomfortable being led into the trackless Huron Mountains by a convicted robber and killer.

Late in life the old stagecoach robber moved to Fort Myers, Florida, where on September 24, 1952, at 86 years of age, he committed suicide.

SILAS DOTY

Michigan's Greatest Thief

Given the choice and means, Silas Doty probably would rather have stolen his mother's milk than simply nurse at her breast. If ever a person was born to steal it was Silas Doty, who first saw the light of day on May 30, 1800, and soon became a one-man crime wave that crested in Michigan and didn't recede until his death in 1876.

Silas stole just about anything from anywhere, leading Michigan poet Will Carleton to call him the "most consummate and unmitigated thief that America has ever produced." If second-hand tooth tartar had commanded a good price, Doty could have scraped it from your molars and been two miles down the road before you realized it was missing.

Doty began his life of crime not long after leaving the womb. Though born into the devout Christian home of a Vermont, farmer, Silas claimed that when he began to crawl he also launched his criminal career by hiding spoons and other small objects under rugs. As a toddler he delighted in stealing from his brothers and sisters, and when Silas reached school age he discovered an even larger world waiting to be filched. In his one-room elementary schoolhouse, nothing was safe from Silas' quick fingers, including his teacher's penknife, which he treasured for years.

Young Doty's small world was by no means oblivious to his worrisome proclivities. His parents knew Silas' fingers were stickier than flypaper and that objects of every description often disappeared in their son's wake. And Doty's elementary-school teacher once bluntly notified the troubled parents that given time, their student in crime would likely nip the entire school from roof beams to chalk slates.

Silas' dad finally snapped when the local blacksmith accused the child of stealing his horseshoes. The elder Doty dragged his son to their barn and threatened to hang him if he didn't tell the truth. When Silas proclaimed his innocence, his father tossed a rope over a beam and looped the noosed end around the child's neck. Dad then grabbed the other end and slowly tightened the noose, pulling Silas within hailing distance of eternity. But when asked again to confess, Silas called his father's bluff and later claimed he considered the episode his baptism into a life of crime.

At age nine, Silas and his family moved to Bangor in upstate New York, where Silas graduated from stealing for amusement to stealing for profit. Each winter, trappers set lines in and around Bangor. Silas learned where the lines ran and when they were checked and simply beat the trappers to their own game. The young crook took the best of the trapped animals, skinned them, and sold the pelts. The cunning nine-year-old left enough game in the traps to avoid suspicion and was thus able to run the operation for three years without detection before moving on to more traditional criminal activities.

At 16, Silas talked a blacksmith into the use of his shop, where he made a number of skeleton keys plus a near-professional set of burglar tools, all of which he used within the year to commit his first burglary. By his own admission, Silas enjoyed success breaking into houses, as well as stealing horses, rustling cattle, shoplifting, and passing counterfeit money — all while a teenager.

He also was still in his teens when he joined a loose network of thieves that operated across the state. His dad didn't threaten to string him up again, but arguments between father and son became commonplace as the elder Doty grew increasingly concerned that the blame for the region's rising crime rate rested squarely on his son's shoulders.

In 1820, tired of the constant parental friction and suspicion, Silas left home and set out for Buffalo, intending to take up sailing as a career. But he quickly took a different yet already familiar tack when, in his view, it seemed all of Buffalo begged to be robbed. Only days after Doty's arrival, good horses disappeared from several barns, and a cash register that went unwatched for a couple of minutes suffered an unscheduled $1,000 withdrawal. His pockets full of money and riding on one of the stolen animals, Doty headed to Rochester, New York, where he sold the horses.

He stole yet another horse for the ride back to Buffalo but hadn't made it out of town before the theft was reported and the call went out to form a posse and give chase. To evade the law, Silas sidetracked to a farm, where he convinced the owner he was a sheriff on the trail of a horse thief and asked if he and his horse might rest awhile. Doty stabled the stolen horse, took a seat in the farm house, and even had the nerve to ask the farmer's wife for a meal. As the young crook was enjoying dinner, his pursuers rode past. When he knew the posse would be well out of the way, Doty saddled his horse and set out for home, carrying away the farmer's wall clock, which he had much admired, under his coat. He further repaid the family's kindness by returning days later and stealing their workhorses.

Back in Buffalo, Doty finally did sign on as a sailor aboard a boat that stopped at every small town along the St. Lawrence River. He quickly became disenchanted with the seaman's life, because he didn't have enough down time in port for thievery. To correct the imbalance, Doty became a one-time pirate. He stole a small boat, loaded it with stolen goods, peddled the merchandise from town to town, then sank the boat.

Silas' criminal exploits also occasionally veered off in other unexpected and surprising directions. Predicting the course of a butterfly within a field of flowers or the path of a tornado would probably have proven easier. After subjecting Boston to a one-man crime wave during a brief visit, Doty — apparently on a whim — picked up a partner named Wicks and then sailed to England, where he became an international criminal before reaching his 25th birthday. In Liverpool the young Americans pulled together a criminal gang that carried out night-time assaults on local shops. With his set of precision burglar tools, Doty picked the stores' locks, after which his crew emptied the premises then locally fenced the goods for quick cash. He also stole a fair amount of Liverpool-area horse flesh and even hatched grand plans for a country-wide theft of horses, which were to be sold in France. But the law was nipping at Doty's heals, so after barely a year in England, he dropped the scheme and sailed back to the states with Wicks.

Surprisingly, Silas returned to the family farm and met and married Sophia Athens in 1825. Though in the first blush of wedded bliss the groom determined to go straight, poor Sophia apparently never figured much in Silas' life, barely rating a mention in his autobiography, even though they had several children together. For Doty, giving up crime would prove harder than an addict kicking heroin. He managed to stay on the straight-and-narrow for only a few post-marital months before giving in to the craving for being on the road and stealing something — hell, anything.

Silas told his young wife he was going sailing, but instead set off on a summer crime spree that tacked back and forth across New England and eastern Canada. In Halifax, Nova Scotia he talked the madam of a whorehouse into helping him rob her patrons in return for a cut of the take. Doty spent the night slipping in and out of bedrooms temporarily occupied by men ill-prepared to thwart a robbery. When Doty finished working the rooms, he slipped into the madam's office, and instead of sharing the proceeds, opened her safe, emptied it of cash and valuables, and fled.

In the winter of 1827 Silas' career took another twist; he played Robin Hood for the first time. He traveled the short distance to Plattsburg, New York, where first he stole a sleigh and a team of horses, then broke into a store and loaded the sleigh with tea, sugar, flour and meat before returning home and sharing his booty with the area's poor.

For the next several years, Doty spent winters on the farm and summers maintaining the fiction of sailing the Great Lakes.

In the spring of 1834, Doty moved to Adrian, Michigan, looking for new criminal opportunities and leaving behind a state where his activities had drawn too much scrutiny. To his delight, Doty found Michigan ripe for the picking and southeastern Michigan teeming with folks living on the wrong side of the law. A quick canvassing of the counties in his area revealed an inept ring of crooks, which Doty took over, boosted membership, shared his expertise, and turned it into a formidable organization of thieves, burglars, counterfeiters, highwaymen, and even killers. Silas Doty had become criminal royalty.

Doty had hardly settled in Adrian, when the smorgasbord of opportunities for ill-gotten gain in more-populated Detroit drew him there for an exploratory visit. Silas decided he needed a good horse to take him to Detroit. He could have bought or rented one from a livery stable, but both of those options were unthinkable, since horses, carriages and buggies topped the list of his favorite things to steal. So he nosed around until he learned of the best piece of horseflesh in his new home area, stole it, and headed for Detroit. En route, however, Doty decided to detour to Port Huron, where he sold the animal for $85 then promptly stole a team of horses and a carriage for the trip back home.

Doty finally did make Detroit in 1835, arriving by boat without committing a felony on the way. He and his sometimes partner in crime, Wicks, planned to check out smuggling opportunities, but instant gratification supplanted long-range plans when the two observed long trains of heavily loaded wagons heading west out of the city on the Chicago Road (future US-12). When the teamsters rendezvoused at Plymouth, Doty and Wicks seized the opportunity to steal one of their wagons, then peddled the goods to Detroit grocery shops.

Following the robbery, Doty remained in Detroit for a couple of years and, foreshadowing the Prohibition Era, made good money smuggling liquor into the city from Canada.

Also during his stay, Doty pulled off one of his most celebrated crimes. Two years before officially being granted statehood, Michigan residents, in anticipation and preparation, approved a constitution and elected legislators. On November 1, 1835, those representatives held a one-day session in Detroit, then adjourned for three months. Most of the politicians remained in town, staying at the United States Hotel and using the time to find trouble and wallow in it. Doty used the time to plan a daring caper. He conscripted a cohort, the hotel's desk clerk, who took a group of legislators on a night of slumming in Detroit's tenderloin district. After a few hours of whoring and drinking, the pols returned to their hotel rooms and passed out. Doty then picked the locks, slipped into the legislators' rooms, and emptied the cash from their pockets. If the politicians noticed an absence of money the next morning, they blamed it on the bordellos they had visited the previous night. There is some uncertainty as to how many rooms Doty broke into that night, but at the very least he made off with $600 from three rooms.

In 1836 Silas paid another visit to Port Huron on yet another stolen horse. This time, however, while Silas ate dinner while awaiting a buyer, a deputy sheriff interrupted the meal by arresting Doty for the theft. But somehow Silas talked the deputy into letting him finish his meal, and while doing so Doty learned the deputy had a sick horse. Telling the lawman he had a gift for doctoring horses, Doty persuaded the deputy to bring him to the stable, where he discovered a horse suffering from colic. Doty purged the animal with whiskey and pepper, which seemed to help.

While ministering to the horse, Doty palmed a trowel blade and slipped it into his clothing. During the night he used the blade to remove the molding and sash from his second-story jail cell's barless window. He next tied sheets and blankets together, anchored one end of the ad hoc rope to a bedpost, and climbed down to freedom. Doty headed straight to the nearest stable, stole a horse, and rode off wrapped in a quilt.

Doty spent most of the next year scouting likely marks while sailing the Great Lakes on passenger boats. When the opportunity presented itself, Doty would pick out a rich pigeon, follow him to his hotel, and break into his room when the man left to eat or stroll the city.

In 1837 Doty left Detroit, rented the Patch Farm near Tecumseh, and swore he'd go straight. And he did ... straight back to stealing. Silas grew obsessed with "obtaining" a superbly matched team of horses he had drooled over since first seeing the animals in Detroit. Doty scratched the itch, but ended up fleeing the city with a posse and a pack of hounds close behind. The chase caromed through Adrian, and Silas didn't finally outrun his pursuers until somewhere in northern Ohio.

Undeterred by the close call or, more likely, simply unable to stop himself, Doty continued to steal because it had become his addiction. He stole anything and everything, including once — for no reason or evident purpose other than to just do it — a paltry 40 bushels of wheat. In 1837 or '38 he made a horse-stealing trip to Kentucky, where he also stole a slave, whom he set free in Ohio. Meanwhile, he continued to work his farm and occasionally showed up in Adrian or Tecumseh, where he took a five-fingered discount on whatever groceries he needed.

But never comfortable in one place for long, Doty moved to yet another farm, in Steuben County in northern Indiana in 1838. He hired Lorenzo G. Noyes as a farmhand, but the two argued constantly. After one especially heated exchange, Noyes quit and stormed off, threatening to tell authorities about Doty's numerous crimes. Silas wasn't about to let Noyes have the last word. Doty followed his hired help down the road, where the two again spewed rage at each other until Silas raised his hickory walking stick and clubbed Noyes over the head with it. When Doty realized the blow had killed Noyes, he dragged his first murder victim to a nearby swamp and buried the body.

While Noyes lay moldering in a shallow, unmarked grave, Doty again crossed state lines and the law but — probably to his surprise as much as anyone else's — was caught, arrested, and tried and convicted for stealing buffalo robes in Michigan. In 1841 Silas was sent to Jackson State Prison, where things were about to get even worse for him. Noyes' body was discovered in 1842, whereupon the Michigan convict was turned over to the State of Indiana to stand trial for the murder.

The trial took place in Angola, Indiana, amid great public excitement. In spite of Doty being generally reviled in the area, the trial resulted in a hung jury. The retrial was moved to Fort Wayne, where the jury returned a verdict of second-degree murder, and Silas was sentenced to life imprisonment. The convict spent a year at hard labor in Jeffersonville, Indiana, while his lawyer appealed the case to the state Supreme Court, which granted Doty a retrial.

Doty was returned to Steuben County for trial, but his lawyer fought for a change of venue to LaGrange County. While waiting to see where he'd eventually end up, Doty put his time to good use. He cut a hole in his second-story cell's floor, dropped through to the ground floor, then ripped through a wall and lit out. He made it as far as Logansport, where he was arrested, handcuffed, and brought to Fort Wayne. But his guards evidently couldn't have kept a goldfish in a bowl. They all fell asleep, allowing Doty to slip out a window. He then stole a canal boat's lead horse and rode for freedom. But again he was apprehended, placed under heavy guard, and returned to the Angola prison. Fed up with Doty's repeated escapes, the Angola jailer fitted the prisoner with a pair of 20-pound ankle bracelets connected by a logging chain.

But within a week Doty broke out, stole a horse, and — still fettered and thus presumably riding sidesaddle — made it to his Steuben County farm. He cut off his constraints with a cold chisel and waited not a second before heading south for the Mexican War and the darkest days of his criminal career.

It wasn't patriotic fervor that led Doty south, but rather the coldly calculated possibility of having his murder charge and life sentence dropped. Congress had just passed a law "forgiving all past offenses to those who enlisted in this war to the end." To give the appearance of complying, Doty wrote home from Texas that he had enlisted in the army for the duration of the war. But that was a load of bull. In reality, Doty hired on as an army cook, slinging hash during the day and reserving evenings for robbery and murder.

Doty followed the army to Vera Cruz, Mexico, where he immediately gathered a crew of cut-throats who began preying on wealthy Mexicans. Silas and his gang would storm a hacienda, line the family up and, after threatening to kill everyone, demand jewels and money. As the front-line U.S. Army troops attacked Monterey, Doty and his gang brought up the rear, looting homes. In Mexico City, Doty found Sunday mornings to be the best times to burglarize wealthy homes because the families were almost certainly at mass.

By his own later admission Doty even became a murderous highwayman. He and a couple of accomplices set up ambushes along lonely stretches of road, waited for a wealthy Mexican to pass by, and then cut the victim down in a hail of bullets. The killers then stripped the body of valuables plus took the horse, saddle, and harness for future sale.

Doty also proved adroit at winning points with the powerful, just in case he ever needed a favor. When Doty discovered one particularly magnificent horse, he promptly stole it and presented it as a gift to General Scott, Commander of the U.S. Army in Mexico. What the general thought of an army cook presenting him with a fine horse, and how an army cook could come into possession of such an animal is lost to history.

In 1848, with Santa Anna and the Mexican Army defeated and the war over, Doty returned to Michigan, this time to Branch County, where he was regarded by most, including the law, as a returning veteran who had earned clemency for any crimes committed before the war.

Silas had a clean sheet but couldn't dirty it fast enough. His consuming need, his addiction, demanded ever-more-frequent fixes. As a result, he embarked on an orgy of stealing — making off with oats, wheat, corn, pork, cattle, harnesses, plows, the contents of entire stores, and once a notions peddler's entire wagon plus his horse. Yes, another horse. Always horses.

Doty's daily need to steal did make him a good neighbor. In fact, you didn't have to want for darn near anything if you lived near Doty. All you had to do was wish out loud in his presence, and sometimes you didn't even have to do that. Once for instance, when he noticed a neighboring family sleeping on the floor, he stole beds from a furniture store and bedding from a Hillsdale hotel then dropped off the surprise gifts at the family's front door. He stole rope, plows, hoes, forks, axes, and gave them to neighbors. When a newly elected state representative complained of having to attend the state legislature in a pair of old boots, Doty measured the man's feet, went to a Coldwater shoe store, stole a pair of fine boots, and sent his representative to Lansing well-shod.

His neighbors' reaction to the bounty of stolen goods that materialized at their front door is unknown, but probably ran from deep appreciation to embarrassment. It's doubtful that Doty himself ever experienced a "warm feeling" for the "good deeds." He only experienced the "warm fuzzies" after stealing a horse. The delivering of free goods to his neighbors, however, did have the practical effect of virtually assuring that they would never testify against him.

Nevertheless, Silas Doty's life of crime did finally catch up to and bury him under a mountain of hard time. In August 1849 he was arrested, brought to Hillsdale County, and charged with, in his own words, "a variety of things too numerous to mention." Instead of swift and sure justice, however, the trial date was set months in the future and the court allowed Doty to make bail. Upon his release, he set off on the biggest crime spree of his life, a binge that took him through Chicago, St. Louis, and into Indiana, where the law again caught up to him in 1851. He was returned to Hillsdale County for a short trial and a long sentence: 17 years of hard labor at Jackson.

The 51-year-old thief got on the good side of his guards, who occasionally allowed him to work outside the walls doing farm chores. The small freedoms also provided Doty with the opportunity to indulge in small-time thievery. He also made a key that unlocked the female wing of

Silas Doty

the prison, where he undoubtedly must have enjoyed visiting. Doty even stole time from the state by cutting two years off his sentence for good behavior.

On September 1, 1866, having served 15 years, Silas walked out of the prison gates a free man but with pockets stuffed with hate. Now a widower (his wife had died while he did time), he returned to Stueben County, Indiana, and stoked his wrath. He swore revenge on at least three men he blamed for his long incarceration and looked forward to killing them. Topping the list was a lawyer from Coldwater.

So off Silas went with murder in his heart. But old habits die hard, and when he reached Coldwater he discovered the man owned a good-looking horse. Now, Silas could have found the man, killed him, and then stolen the horse, but that would have postponed gratification for his #1 favorite activity. So Silas stole the horse and rode off, intending to some day return and rub out the owner. But Doty had hardly gotten a "yahoo!" past his throat before he was nabbed with the stolen animal. Hello again Jackson, this time for a three-year stretch.

Released again in 1870, Doty managed to steer clear of the law for a couple of years until he decided to take a northern boat trip to reinvigorate his aging body. But damned if he didn't find himself disembarking from the boat with a "large and valuable valise stuck to (his) hand." Problem was, the police also found him with the valise, which had been reported stolen. To the surprise of many, Doty pleaded guilty and received two more years in prison. Another author has speculated that at age 70, Doty simply considered Jackson home and committed a crime to get a ticket back.

In 1875 Silas Doty walked out of prison for the last time at age 75 and settled in Hillsdale County, where he planned to fully immerse himself in criminal activities. He took a young partner, and when he discovered the kid was double-crossing him, Doty briefly contemplated murder. Instead, the old crook retired and spent his last year thumbing his nose at society by chronicling his complete lack of respect for law-abiding America and its rules and laws in his autobiography. Silas Doty stole out of this world on March 15, 1876, at Reading, Michigan.

Doty's funeral drew a huge crowd, and *The Hillsdale Standard* in its obituary noted, "There seemed to be an innate principle in his nature which caused him to make frequent peculations on the rights of others, which led him into frequent trouble and many years imprisonment in the various 'reformatory' institutions of the country.

Notwithstanding his many depredations on the property of others, which caused him to be an object of fear to the law-abiding citizens in the neighborhood in which he might be staying, he was not without noble traits of character and he is reported to have many times relieved the wants of suffering even if in doing so he was obliged to commit an act upon which jeopardized his personal liberty."

In the years following Silas' death, his family attempted to reform and refurbish the tarnished image of their ancestor. They refused to talk about his crimes except for detailing his stealing to help the poor. Some in the family even claimed that Doty's autobiography was in fact written by one of his gang so that the ghostwriter could lay many of his crimes on Silas' doorstep. When the autobiography was published in 1880, the Doty family made a concerted effort to prevent the public from seeing it by buying all copies they could find and destroying them.

Ironically, history is one of the few things Silas never attempted to steal. He left that to his family.

THE McDONALDS

The Day Justice Went Wild in Menominee

Frank McDonald and John McDougal failed to understand that courting trouble was a lot like a male Black Widow spider courting a mate — when you're most passionately engaged, violence, like the female spider, will turn and eat you alive.

When the two arrived in Menominee from Ontario in the late 1870s, the city was a bustling seaport and lumber town. By 1881 more than 30 sawmills ripped logs into timber along the Menominee River, and the town billed itself as the world's largest lumber port. Located on the southernmost tip of the U.P., the town also had its rough edges, but Marinette, Wisconsin, on the south bank of the Menominee River, boasted a worse reputation. That changed in one night when ad hoc justice was doled out to Frank and John — cousins raised as brothers and generally known as "the McDonalds."

In 1880 the boys spent three days in jail on a drunk and disorderly charge. Drunk and disorderly! To two of the toughest men in the north woods, that was not a punishable offense, it was a career move. The McDonalds were insulted by the incarceration. So upon their release they purchased the kind of cutlery meant to open wounds rather than butter toast and promised trouble the next time the law crossed their path.

The law, in the person of Sheriff Julius Reprecht, was not long in coming. The cousins went to work for the Girard Lumber Company, near Menominee, and within a few days had raised enough hell that a shout went out for Reprecht to come and get the drunken thugs and throw them in jail. When Frank and John discovered the sheriff had been summoned, they waylaid Reprecht and beat the sap out of him.

After easing his bruised body back to Menominee, the sheriff deputized George Kittson and sicced him on the McDonalds. George stood over six feet tall, weighed 200 pounds, and was tougher than hob-nailed boots. Kittson returned to the lumber camp, took the cousins by surprise, and brought them back to Menominee in chains. The two thugs were found guilty of resisting arrest and assaulting the sheriff, and sentenced to a year and a half in Jackson State Prison.

The cousins spent the 12 months they served burning for revenge. Upon their release, Frank, 23, and John, 27, returned to Menominee to discover Reprecht would not suffer from their slowly basted hate. Defeated in a re-election bid, the former sheriff had left town. But George Kittson was still around.

On September 26, 1881, the booze-fueled McDonalds entered the Montreal Bar to top off their alcohol blood levels. The pair found Norman Kittson, George's brother, tending bar and taunted him with details of how George would pay for arresting them. Tired of goading Norman, the pair decided they needed some female companionship and knew right where it could be purchased. The Three Chimneys Whorehouse was just a short walk away, and the cousins couldn't believe their luck when they also found yet another Kittson brother, Billy, drinking there.

The well-lubricated McDonalds began baiting Billy (who was also well into his cups). Voices rose, tempers rose, and a whiskey bottle levitated, which Billy broke over the prow of Frank's head, christening the younger cousin with whiskey and launching a one-sided fight.

Billy staggered out of the Three Chimneys, probably on his way to the Montreal House to get reinforcements, followed by the whiskey-soaked and by now murderous McDonalds. Norm had stepped out of the Montreal House and was standing on the corner near the saloon when he saw his brother heading his way with the McDonalds in pursuit. Norm shouted a warning to Billy who replied, "I'm not afraid of those sons of bitches."

Norm then flung a half-pleading, half-threatening, "Don't do nothin' boys," at the cousins. John McDougal answered by grabbing a peavey, a stout wooden pole used for handling logs, and with a Sammy Sosa swing, knocking Billy to his hands and knees. The oldest cousin then slipped a six-inch knife from its hiding place and buried it to the hilt in Billy's back. Norm sped to his brother's aid only to receive a gruesome slash to the neck from the knife-wielding Frank. Knocked to the ground by the force of the blow, Norm pulled a gun and fired wildly at the attackers, hitting Frank in the meaty part of his calf. As Norm was drawing his weapon, Billy had struggled back to two feet and went to help his brother only to be stabbed again, this time in the head. Frank's wounding, however, ended the vicious fight, and the McDonalds stole a buggy and headed for medical help.

Bloodied Billy, probably kept upright by liquor, wobbled into the Montreal House and ordered a round for the crowd. He raised his hands over his head, as if in victory, then fell to the floor dead.

Meanwhile, the McDonalds barged into Dr. Phillip's office and ordered him to patch up Frank's leg. The pair then headed out of town, but Sheriff Barclay quickly caught up and arrested them for first-degree murder. To ensure that witnesses to the murder would be on hand to testify, rather than drift off into the woods, the sheriff locked up a handful in the same jail.

Talk of lynching began as soon as the door clanked shut on the Mc-Donalds' jail cell. That night at a memorial service for President Garfield — who had died the week before after being shot July 2 — the crowd turned ugly, with much talk of instant justice for the two cousins. It came to nothing though, probably because of a lack of alcohol to further fuel and ignite passions.

The next day, at an inquest into Billy Kittson's death, Coroner Henry Nason had to call a quick end to the proceeding and send the McDonalds back to jail when those in attendance roared for blood.

Watching even the short inquest evidently made the audience thirsty, because after Nason adjourned the hearing, the crowd adjourned to Forvilly's Hotel across the river in Marinette. There the owner, Max Forvilly, liberally doused the men with free liquor and urged them to teach the Mc-Donalds a lesson. One man named Stephenson said he'd volunteer a rope, and another otherwise upstanding citizen said he'd provide a timber that would knock down the jail door. Some claimed, long after the fact, that the authorities knew of the brewing lawlessness and asked the local chapter of the Grand Army of the Republic (veterans of the Civil War) to help guard the jail. If asked, the G.A.R. declined.

By nightfall the Forvilly Hotel crowd had turned into an out-of-control, drunken mob that, led by Max, stormed the jail. They battered down the door, pushed Deputy Sheriff Fryer and another deputy aside (as Fryer's wife looked on), grabbed the keys, and opened the cousins' cell.

The McDonalds weren't about to die without a fight. From somewhere Frank pulled a small knife and stabbed the first man to reach him. The next man into the cell knocked Frank to the floor with a blow from an ax. The men were dragged outside, and in the struggle John was thrown over an iron gate, where his neck got caught on a post and was stretched near the breaking point before he was freed.

Some claim both men were dead by the time they reached the street, but other witnesses said that one of the McDonalds pleaded for a priest, who was promptly brought to the scene. By the time Father Heliard of St. John's Church arrived, the men were lying in the mud, with nooses encircling their necks and the other ends of the ropes tied to a horse-drawn wagon. Fr. Heliard tried to reason with the lynch mob, and when reason failed he hurled a curse at the ringleaders, promising they would "die with their boots on." In response, someone pushed the priest to the side of the street, and the driver of the wagon whipped the horse.

As the McDonalds' bodies carved parallel furrows in the muddy street, church bells peeled and mill whistles blew. Parents lifted children onto their shoulders to watch the grizzly spectacle, and here and there, alcohol-emboldened lumberjacks ran out into the street and — to the crowd's screams of approval — kicked the bodies.

By the time the gruesome parade reached the railroad tracks, John and Frank were definitely both long dead. But that didn't matter to the mob. They strung the cousins' lifeless bodies up on the railroad crossing sign and pelted them with stones, sticks, and anything else that came to hand. Finally, Sam Peltier, the owner of a track-side saloon, appeared and asked the mob to stop, complaining the corpses would not only hurt his business but they would scare women, children, and horses.

Well bless their hearts; maybe the mob did care about the feelings of women, children and horses. More likely, the mob concurred with an idea one of the drunken curs came up with for the event's *piece de resistance*. The bodies were cut down, and the macabre procession moved on to the Three Chimneys Whorehouse, where the whole sorry affair had begun. There the mob tossed the cousins' bodies onto beds, then forced some of the unluckier employees to get into bed with the corpses. The mob then dragged the McDonalds' lifeless bodies back outside, rehung them from a pine tree next to Three Chimneys, and torched the bordello.

One of the biggest mysteries surrounding this horrible affair was the whereabouts that evening of Sheriff Barclay. One source claims the lawman owned a stable in town and, unaware of the potential for violence, simply spent the evening at his place of business. However, it's simply unbelievable that the sheriff hadn't heard the talk of lynching and out of the most meager sense of duty would not be guarding his prisoners. It appears he purposefully absented himself from anything to do with the murderous goings on, perhaps out of fear for his own life.

The aftermath to the mob rule proved almost as as devoid of the rule of law as the lynching. Max Forvilly, the most visible of the lynch mob's ringleaders was arrested but never stood trial. In fact, neither he nor anyone else spent a night in jail, and no one else was even charged with participating in the lynching. The Escanaba *Iron Post* heaped contempt on those responsible for maintaining law and order in Menominee, but then couldn't make up its mind whether or not to disapprove of the actual lynching. Their October 1st edition ended a brief story of the hanging with, "the law itself does not provide adequate punishment for murder — the officers of the law do not succeed in enforcing even the poor penalties prescribed — the jails do not hold the criminals committed to them, and affairs like that of Tuesday night follow."

The next issue of the paper got some facts wrong, plus again slipped into editorializing by printing, "Rumor has it that the individuals who composed the Menominee mob are 'wanted' by authorities; that they are to be arrested, tried and punished, if the 'army of Michigan' has to be mobilized and sent ... to aid ... the sheriff. We imagine it will have to come. If the sheriff ... could not stand off the mob and keep his prisoners, he is not likely to make much of a success of arresting the same crowd now. There are men with sand in their craws in Menominee, but they were not on guard at the jail the night the McDonalds were hanged."

And what of the priest's curse? Various sources delight in enumerating the many compliant conveyances by which the mob leaders passed on. Max Forvilly reportedly went insane, and the man who hit Frank with the ax died sitting under a tree — drum roll, please — with his boots on. Others in the mob respectively drowned, died of a knife wound, and succumbed in a sawmill accident. Even taken together, however, the deaths seem poor proof of the curse's validity. After all, all men employed in the lumber industry in the late 19th century had a better than fair chance of dying with their boots on. The northern Michigan lumber frontier found many ways to make widows.

Dan Seavey

Lake Michigan Pirate

Captain Dan Seavey never made anyone walk the plank, never hoisted the skull and crossbones, and never had a peg leg or a parrot, but there was enough swash and buckle in this waterborne outlaw's life to rank with the best of his more-famous Caribbean predecessors. Seavey's skullduggery variously included smuggling liquor, turning his boat into a whorehouse and a gambling casino, boat theft, common thievery, poaching and murder.

As with most pirate stories, it's sometimes difficult to separate fact from the fanciful, and there seems to be at least two versions of nearly every major event in Seavey's life. But one thing's certain: unlike the majority of pirates who sailed the Caribbean during the great age of piracy in the 17th and 18th centuries, Dan Seavey didn't end up with a noose around his neck.

The future Great Lakes pirate slipped into this world on March 23, 1865, in Portland, Maine. Even as a boy, sailing came second nature to Seavey, who ran away from home at 13 and went to sea on tramp steamers. While still in his teens he also signed up for a stint in the navy. After serving out his enlistment, Dan headed west and worked for the Bureau of Indian Affairs in Wisconsin and Minnesota before returning to the water as a commercial fisherman and fish-market owner in Milwaukee. He gave up the sea again when he married and had a daughter. Some claim Seavey also owned at least two bars and a farm, that is until gold fever infected him and he cast aside everything, including his family, to join the Alaska Gold Rush.

When his fever broke, so was Seavey. Pockets empty, he returned from Alaska in the late 1800s and drifted to Escanaba. There, legitimately or otherwise, Dan acquired a trim, little two-masted schooner, the *Wanderer*, and announced he was starting a small freight-boat service that would take anything to any port on Lake Michigan.

In reality the business served as cover for piracy. Seavey and a small crew would silently slip the *Wanderer*, with no running lights, into ports in the dead of night and make off with anything on wharves, in unlocked warehouses, or on nearby streets that was of value and could be carried on the schooner. On one occasion, they crept into a port, loaded the *Wanderer* with lumber that had been awaiting the arrival of another schooner, and after transferring the wood, Dan noticed two oxen staked out on the wharf. He had the crew drive the animals on board, figuring the oxen could be helpful in unloading the lumber. If not, they could be eaten.

Another one of Seavey's favorite enterprises was to pluck cargo from boats that had been driven ashore by storms, poor seamanship, or other fates of the sea. As the ships foundered on rocks and sandbars, they were often abandoned by their crews, and under maritime law, their cargo became free pickings for salvagers like Seavey.

If shipwrecks weren't occurring frequently enough, Dan would take matters into his own hands by extinguishing the lights on navigation buoys and replacing the disabled markers with fakes. Invariably, Dan's improvised navigational aids would lead an unsuspecting Great Lakes freighter onto the rocks or aground instead of to a safe harbor. Dan stayed out of sight until the freighter's crew left their foundering boat then retrieved his false buoys and had his crew salvage the cargo.

Although Seavey occasionally returned to Escanaba with his plunder, he most often disposed of it in Chicago, where a large criminal underworld didn't inquire about bills of lading and other potentially embarrassing details. Dan could tie up to any dock in Chicago carrying anything from clothes to caviar and find a no-questions-asked buyer.

Seavey also added another unique line item to his resume — poaching. Now, poaching and piracy are seldom spoken of in the same breath. Blackbeard didn't earn his fearful reputation by hunting out-of-season, and Long John Silver didn't search out Treasure Island because of its valuable deer herd. Pirate Dan Seavey, however, poached deer and did so very profitably. In fact, shortly after the turn of the 20th century, Seavey monopolized the Chicago venison market. Venison was in especially great demand during the fall months, and Dan met all orders by "harvesting" deer from a large herd on Summer Island, just off the Garden Peninsula. Seavey packed the *Wanderer* with iced venison and delivered the meat to a wholesale company controlled by Chicago's criminal element.

The company, however, soon decided to increase their profits by directly handling the poaching and butchering side of the lucrative, illegal operation. So they launched a genuine hostile takeover by sending a boatload of thugs north to Summer Island. There, the Chicago gang overpowered and drove off Seavey and his crew, took over the processing of the deer, loaded their boat with venison, and set sail for Chicago. But Seavey wasn't about to let a gang of city slickers run him off his own territory. From somewhere the fearless captain appropriated a small cannon and mounted it on the Wanderer. The Windy City crew was still far from home when the *Wanderer* sailed over the horizon and closed with their craft. When the *Wanderer* ran out a newly installed cannon, the Chicago toughs realized they were suddenly and regretfully on the wrong end of an arms race. Dan Seavey became the first and only pirate on the Great Lakes to sink another boat with cannon fire.

At least once — and more likely, regularly — Seavey turned the *Wanderer* into a floating whorehouse. One Charlevoix man, during his latter years, recalled that he had watched the *Wanderer* — probably headed for the sexually undernourished lumberjacks of East Jordan and Boyne City — sail up the Pine River and pass under the bridge into Round Lake with a boatload of "tarts" lining the gunwales and showing off their wares. Seavey, however, never tied up to a dock when the *Wanderer* lifted her skirts and entertained men, but instead cautiously anchored off shore and brought customers aboard by dory.

The *Wanderer* also regularly resupplied "Squeaky Swartz's" Frankfort bordello with "soiled doves." And after dropping off the fresh faces, Seavey often loaded up women who'd had the shine worn off at Squeaky's and transported them to the Soo area, where a new clientele eagerly awaited them.

For many men, on the other hand, boarding the *Wanderer* was reputedly the last voyage they ever took. It was long suspected by contemporaries but never proved that easy marks, probably more often drunk than not, were lured aboard the *Wanderer* as she set sail and were later tossed overboard with their pockets turned inside out. The persistency of the rumors may be due in part to Captain Dan's greatest act of piracy, the taking of the *Nellie Johnson.*

The *Nellie Johnson* was a stout, little schooner that sailed out of Beaver Island. One night as the *Johnson* snuggled-up to a Charlevoix dock, Dan drank the schooner's crew under the table at a local saloon. Leaving the crew in an alcoholic stupor, Seavey boarded the *Johnson*, subdued the captain, and set sail for Chicago. Somewhere out in Lake Michigan the captain was tossed over the side and was never seen again. In the Windy City, Seavey quickly found a buyer for the boat and its cargo.

It's likely Seavey pirated another Great Lakes schooner prior to the *Nellie Johnson.* Years after the alleged incident, old-timers talked of a schooner and its cargo that Seavey stole from a Chicago wharf and sailed across Lake Michigan with the law close behind. Dan raced the stolen boat into Frankfort harbor without reducing an inch of canvas, ran the vessel aground, and jumped ashore and disappeared.

Although Seavey and his exploits had become the stuff of legend in waterfront dives, saloons, and among the criminal element around northern Lake Michigan, he had somehow escaped serious attention from the law enforcement community. But open piracy got everyone's attention, finally even that of the law. The *U.S.S. Tuscarora*, a motorized federal revenue cutter, caught up with Seavey as he was single-handedly sailing, for hire, a pleasure yacht from Frankfort to Mackinaw. It's unclear whether the cutter's captain was tipped off as to Seavey's whereabouts or, as some have suggested, the pirate's arrest on board the yacht was the culmination of an elaborate law-enforcement sting operation. After a spirited race between sail and steam power, Seavey was arrested and taken to Chicago.

At his trial for piracy in Chicago, Captain Dan claimed that the Captain of the *Nellie Johnson*, while drunk, gave the schooner and cargo to him as payment for an old debt. Since the one person who could refute the claim wasn't alive, Seavey walked free. However, rumors widely circulated that Dan had escaped a guilty verdict because he had been deputized as a U.S. Marshall.

It's true that shortly after the trial Dan sported a U.S. Marshall's badge, but most likely because officials decided that if they couldn't put Seavey behind bars they'd put him out of business by hiring him to stop whiskey smuggling, the illegal venison trade, and piracy around the Great Lakes. As it turned out, when Seavey gave up his criminal activities, that alone caused a significant drop in the crime rate in and around Lake Michigan. And because of his toughness, just the knowledge that Seavey was on the right side of the law was enough to inspire other seafaring criminals to re-think their calling.

Both throughout his criminal years and after he started wearing a badge, Dan Seavey was a much-admired and well-liked man who was even looked upon by some as a living legend. Children especially seemed to naturally gravitate to Seavey. The pirate let them hang out on his boat and was generous with fresh fruit when carried as cargo.

Seavey usually spent winters in Escanaba, where many of the town's boys looked on him with near hero worship. One father, however, who was not pleased that his son spent so much time with and emulated such a shady character, one day waited near the end of the dock for the child to leave the *Wanderer*. The father caught his son at the foot of the dock, bent him over his knee, and began administering a public spanking. Corporal punishment was still being applied when Seavey grabbed the father's shoulder, spun him around, and threw the surprised dad over his knee. As Seavey's large hand walloped the father's derriere, he gruffly ordered the stunned parent to, "Leave my shipmates alone."

During sailing season, when reaching Charlevoix, Frankfort, Menom-inee, Escanaba and other ports and not bent on thievery, a saloon was in-variably Dan's first stop. He often treated the house to a round, enjoyed both telling and hearing a good story, and often broke up a bar full of drunks with his sense of humor. During his bar crawls, for instance, he often carried a flour sack filled with skulls, which he took great delight in slipping onto the bar next to the glass of drunks whose attention had been momentarily diverted. When the barflies turned back to their drinks and found a human skull grinning at them, the reaction ranged from passing out to passing water to running from the saloon in terror. It was always en-tertaining and even rehabilitative, when one grateful woman offered

Seavey money as thanks for scaring her husband into renouncing booze.

But above all else Captain Dan Seavey loved to fight. He was a terrific brawler who paid no attention to the Marquis of Queensbury's damnfool rules. Seavey, like most other northern Michigan fighters, subscribed to simpler strictures: no knifing, no gun play, and as long as you used only your bare hands and teeth, you could tear your opponent limb from limb, or proceed vigorously toward that goal until he cried "uncle."

Dan would go anywhere for a fight, and if he heard a new tough man had shown up in a port he frequented, Seavey would drop everything and make sail for the town. When news that a fighter with a reputation had shown up in Manistee, he lost no time in reaching that port and going from saloon to saloon looking for the man. When Dan finally located the fighter, the two of them ordered everyone else out of the place and went at each other like caged roosters. They had nearly destroyed the saloon before the police arrived and stopped the fight. Word spread that Dan appeared to be getting the best of the new man when the fight was interrupted.

In 1904 Seavey challenged Mitch Love, reputed to be a "hell of a fighter," to a match in Frankfort simply to see who was the best brawler. The fight was scheduled for winter and attracted a large crowd, mostly men from town plus throughout the rest of northern Michigan. The bare-knuckled contest — held within a circle drawn on the ice in Frankfort harbor — dragged on for two tortuous hours before friends carried Love from the ice, and Seavey stood bloodied but triumphant.

The only man Seavey couldn't lick was a compact firecracker who showed up at the dock in Escanaba and taunted Dan into stepping ashore for a fight. The Captain couldn't lay a hand on the smaller man, who darted in and out and puffed Dan's eyes and bloodied his lips with lightening-quick fists. When Seavey got mad the beating got worse, with the bigger man ending up on his hands and knees, leaking blood from numerous wounds, swearing a blue streak, and unable to get to his feet. Dan never found out that local men had set him up by importing a professional fighter from Chicago to teach the captain a little humility.

But to Dan, hell it didn't matter if he got beat; he still loved a good fight and so challenged the little man to a rematch the next day. But the man left town, never to be seen again.

Even his appointment as deputy U.S. Marshall didn't end Dan's fighting days, and on occasion, his arrest of a lawbreaker turned into as great an exploit as his old piracy escapades.

The most celebrated story chronicles the time when, not long after his appointment as a lawman, Seavey's superiors aimed him at a trader known for smuggling whiskey to the Indians in the U.P. The newly minted lawman caught up with his man in a Naubinway bar. When Seavey informed the smuggler he was under arrest, the man replied, "If you can drag me outside, I'll board your schooner for Chicago." Seavey must have been delighted to find that law enforcement could be so damn much fun. The marshall readily agreed to the challenge and had a couple of celebratory drinks with his adversary before they went at it. Those present remember the brawl as going on for what seemed like forever, with the combatants occasionally calling a truce and downing a glass of whiskey before pitching into each other again. Dan finally floored his man but felt he needed another injection of whiskey in order to get the smuggler out the door. Not wanting to give the man the advantage of a drink or allow him back on his feet, Dan pinned him to the floor by propping a piano on his neck. Then when refreshed, Dan lifted the piano off the smuggler and, on second thought, offered him a last drink before dragging him from the saloon. The smuggler, however, didn't respond, didn't get up, and never got up. He died the next day. Seavey filed a report but was never questioned about the incident.

It's not known how long Dan served as a deputy Marshall, but he reputedly was still picking fights in bars at the age of 60.

Seavey's life as a pirate was long and profitable, and some have speculated that he earned an unbelievable, unconfirmed and, frankly, unsupported million dollars as an outlaw. Whatever the amount, no one's sure what happened to it. Some have bestowed a Robin Hood reputation on Seavey, saying he gave most of his money to unspecified "poor and children." No one has reported legends or rumors of buried treasure.

One thing certain, he didn't take it with him to the grave. Captain Dan Seavey, the last of his kind, died a pauper in a convalescent home in Peshtigo, Wisconsin on February 14, 1949.

JOHN SMALLEY

The Whiskered Train Robber

L ooking back on a string of events that included a daring train robbery,
the murder of a policeman, a frantic manhunt, and a deadly shootout,
the *Clare Sentinel* declared on August 30, 1895, that "Michigan during the
past two weeks has furnished a series of startling tragedies, all related, that
read like the events of a western frontier." The trigger behind the "wild
west" fusillade of violence was one man — John Smalley.

Smalley was born in the early 1860s in Isabella County and was later
tempered — until he could be honed to a fine edge of toughness — in that
area's lumber camps. Those who remembered Smalley's lumbering days
recalled a dangerous brawler and a deadly shot. At some point, Smalley
decided to knock over banks and trains rather than trees, whereupon he
became the most successful and prolific train robber in state history.
Smalley owed his success and longevity at that career, in part, to the fact
he rarely pulled a robbery close to home. His "business trips" took him as
far afield as Nebraska, where he robbed the Union Pacific Railroad, and
Oklahoma, where he and a gang he had assembled carried out at least one
train robbery. After a job, Smalley's gang — which may have included his
younger brother, but whose identities were never revealed or discovered
— would split up, return to Michigan by train, and disappear to their separate hideouts.

Smalley had probably already found his calling as an armed robber
when he set up housekeeping in Brinton, in northern Isabella County,
around 1882. The townspeople soon noted that the father of six often left
home for a week or two, had plenty of money, and was closed-mouth
about his business. But the people of Brinton must have known how to
mind their own business, or Smalley wouldn't have lived there for 10

years. When his wife died in 1892, he pulled up stakes and moved 30 miles north to McBain where he married Cora Brown, or took her as his common-law wife. It appears that the children went to live with their mother's side of the family, because they were never seen in McBain.

Though a McBain neighbor claimed that no member of Cora Brown's family was ever known to do a day's work, the Smalleys may in fact have been a two-income family. Prior to (and possibly after) living with Smalley, Cora had been a successful businesswoman who set up shop in great tent cities that sprang up each summer when the vast expanse of blueberry bushes that proliferated in the lumbered-out and burned-over plains of northern Michigan became heavy with fruit. Hundreds of families camped beside the extensive berry patches and earned badly needed cash picking the fruit and shipping it downstate.

Cora, however, didn't pick blueberries. She found an even-more-fruitful way of making money without leaving her tent. Hell, without even getting out of bed. She was a hard-working and well-known prostitute whose specially marked place of business stood out from the garden-variety working girls' tents in the sea of canvas stretched taut next to the largest berry patches. Cora attached a square of black cloth, rotated to look like a diamond, to her tent flap. The logo led to Cora being nicknamed "Black Diamond," and over time the large, annual campground on the Muskegon River in Missaukee County where Cora conducted most of her business became known as "Diamond City."

Not long after John and Cora began living together, they struck out for Pond Creek, Oklahoma, but the move didn't stick and within months the couple bounced back to McBain. Smalley took up where he left off, robbing trains and the occasional bank and then returning to either McBain and Cora or, more often, to a lonely cabin somewhere near Clare that served as his hideout.

Also upon returning to Michigan, however, Smalley made two career-ending mistakes. First, he began working close to home, and second, he never wore a disguise or even pulled a bandanna up over his face.

And in neither bearing nor looks did Smalley blend in with a crowd. He stood out wherever he went. The desperado was 180 pounds of muscle and sinew spring-loaded into a 5', 8" frame, with a deep, powerful chest flanked by muscular arms. Blue eyes, a broad forehead, a prodigious nose, and a carved-out-of-granite square jaw (evident even beneath a full beard) defined his face. And year round, Smalley wore a black slouch hat and a long, dark, loose overcoat that concealed his constant companions, a pair of revolvers worn on the waist that could be quickly drawn through the coat's cut away pockets.

Yep, Smalley was damn near impossible to overlook, and his first brush with the law should have told him that. In 1893 he robbed a train in Kendalville, Indiana, which was major news during the time and so made the newspaper in Cadillac, Michigan. While en route home, Smalley took a room in that city's American House hotel, where he came face to face with the owner, Orrin Dunham, who also happened to be county sheriff. Dunham, thinking of the train robbery, either intuitively felt that Smalley was a suspicious character, or the newspaper had given at least a partial description of the bandits and the whiskered guy in the long, dark overcoat looked like a match, so the lawman arrested him.

When the sheriff searched his suspect, he discovered that Smalley gave new meaning to the term "packing iron." The outlaw's valise contained $1,700 and eight handguns, plus two more revolvers and a cartridge belt hung from his waist. Dunham wired an inquiry to police in Kendalville but didn't receive a reply. Since it wasn't against the law to carry around $1,700, all the sheriff could do was fine Smalley for carrying concealed weapons and then let him walk.

Next time Smalley crossed paths with the law, he wasn't so fortunate.

On August 20, 1895, as a Chicago & West Michigan Railroad passenger train approached a long curve two miles north of Fennville, in Allegan County, engineer Zibbel saw a lantern swinging across the tracks. Zibbel leaned into the brake handle, but the engine pushed into a pile of ties laid across the tracks before coming to a complete stop, whereupon a man jumped into the cab and pointed a gun at Zibbel and his fireman.

From the baggage car, Conductor E. E. Rice stepped out onto a platform to inquire about the stop and saw a man running toward him. When Rice asked what the man wanted, the reply — punctuated with two shots — was, "You'll find out if you don't get out of the way." Incredulous, Rice called out again and got the same answer, only this time he could feel the bullets rip by his head. He stepped back into the baggage car, locked the door, and told the baggage man they were being robbed.

A moment of silence was followed by a roar that rent the night air as the door of the baggage coach blew off. The man, later identified as Smalley, leaped into the car, held a gun to Rice's head, and ordered him to open the safe. Rice told Smalley there was nothing in it, and in response a third member of the gang took out a stick of dynamite, whittled down one end so it fit into the safe's lock, and lit the fuse. The second explosion in almost as many minutes revealed a safe as empty as Scrooge's heart.

Disgusted that he had come up empty-handed, Smalley began patting down the conductor, and the word aplomb discovered a new synonym that night — E.E. Rice. The man had been shot at twice, nearly been blown up, watched his safe dynamited, and had a gun jammed into his face while being searched. His response? While being relieved of the $7 or $8 cash he carried, Rice commiserated with the robber telling him, "This is a pretty tough business to be in, partner." Smalley agreed saying, "Yes and pretty dangerous, too, but we've got to have money." But when Smalley lifted Rice's watch, the conductor objected, telling the robber he needed the timepiece for his job. The highwayman gave the watch a glance and handed it back to Rice.

Meanwhile, at the rear of the train, brakeman Timothy Murphy headed back down the tracks carrying a red lantern to stop any approaching trains. A voice from the darkness, however, ordered him back, and pistol fire hurried him along. One of the rounds struck Murphy in the lower ribs, but the wound wasn't serious enough to keep the brakeman from returning to the train.

In the coaches, pandemonium had broken out. Most of the passengers were bound for northern Michigan resorts, and hearing indiscriminate gunfire and feeling explosions rock the train was not the way they had expected to begin their vacations. Passengers dived beneath the seats to escape the shots, and as the Grand Rapids *Evening News* later reported, "there was a mad scramble for hiding places for valuables of all kinds and many of the women were in hysterics."

The second robber at the baggage car did suggest the gang rob the passengers, but Smalley said, "No, we been here too damn long now." They did, however, relieve the engineer of a $150 watch plus a few dollars here and there from the rest of the crew before they slipped away in the dark.

Awakened by the sounds of the robbery, an Allegan County Deputy Sheriff in Fennville hastily recruited a posse and was on the outlaws' trail by early morning. And since none of the robbers wore masks, the posse and every other lawman in Michigan had an accurate description of the gang, also by morning.

For two days, posses scoured southwestern Michigan. Sightings of suspicious characters came from all points of the compass, but Smalley and gang eluded capture. On Wednesday, August 22nd, ticket agent C. H. Shirley thought he recognized one of the train robbers when two men — one of whom was heavily bearded and wore a soft slouch hat and long, dark overcoat — bought tickets from him at the Bridge Street Station in Grand Rapids. Shirley telephoned the police.

Four officers responded to the call, raced ahead to the next station on the line, boarded the train, and divided themselves one each among the train's four passenger cars. Officer George Powers, a 52-year-old Civil War veteran considered fearless by his fellow officers, drew the smoking car. He stepped into the front of the compartment as the train got underway, and there sat Smalley in his trademark outfit. The lawman stepped over to the outlaw and asked him where he had boarded the train. Hearing Bridge Street, Powers reached for the valise on Smalley's lap with one hand while his other moved toward the overhead emergency brake chord.

In a blur of motion, Smalley's hand dived into his coat pocket and came out with a gun. He stood up, brought the revolver to bear, and shot Powers in the face. As the policeman was blasted backward, he grabbed the emergency chord, locking the train's brakes. The wheels screeched in sympathy and brought the train to a halt, but not before Smalley and a cohort, probably his brother, bailed out and disappeared. Powers died that night with his wife by his side.

Powers' murder sparked a furious manhunt, but again Smalley proved as hard to find as a plain, uncontestable fact in a presidential debate. Rumors flew across the state by telegraph and telephone, pinpointing the train robbers as variously being in the Muskegon area then Farwell, or that the killer appeared in Evert.

But Smalley somehow made it the hundred or so miles from Grand Rapids to McBain unnoticed. On August 25, when he and an unidentified companion stepped off the 3:10 train in McBain, not surprisingly several of his hometown locals recognized him and had already mentally linked the desperado to the train robbery and the murder of the policeman in Grand Rapids. Word of Smalley's presence in town quickly reached ex-sheriff Gillis McBain, who knew better than to try and take the killer by himself. He called Sheriff Tenant at Lake City, but the lawman was out of the office. Several phone calls later, McBain reached deputy sheriff Bert Spafford in Cadillac, who left immediately and arrived in McBain shortly before nightfall.

Meanwhile, after leaving the train, Smalley had stopped off at Stewart's Saloon for a drink before heading over to Cora Brown's house on Hemlock Street. At another saloon, the young man who had ridden the train with Smalley was observed tipping back a beer before he disappeared, never to be seen again. Many believe he was Smalley's younger brother.

Upon Spafford's arrival, he and ex-sheriff McBain deputized four men, armed the posse with Winchester rifles, and headed for the Brown house. Well, "house" may be too generous a term — the dwelling was actually a one-room shanty with a lean-to propped against the outside back wall. At about 8 p.m. the posse carefully approached the residence, where they saw Smalley sitting on a chair three feet inside the open front door talking with Cora, her mother, brother and a couple of friends. It was dusk, and a lantern lighting the inside of the shanty probably prevented the outlaw from spotting any movement in the growing dark.

The two lawmen detailed a man to watch each side of the building, and as reported in the Grand Rapids *Evening News*, McBain and Spafford then "approached the front door nearly side by side with rifles at their shoulders, covering Smalley who did not see them until the muzzles of the guns were staring him in the face."

Within feet of the front door McBain shouted, "Throw up your hands, Smalley!" The first word had hardly escaped the lawman's mouth before Smalley leaped to his feet, reached for his revolvers, and kicked the door shut. The lawmen responded by opening fire at the closed door, blowing it off its hinges.

Simultaneously, someone doused the light, and everyone in the house but Smalley burst out the back door. An uneasy quiet descended on the scene. Nothing could be heard coming from inside the house, even after one of the sheriffs twice called for Smalley to give himself up. The women had remained nearby to watch, and when McBain asked one of them to go back into the house, relight the lantern, and convince Smalley to surrender, she told the sheriff to "go to hell."

Finally a member of the posse volunteered to inch up to the front door and take a look. He saw Smalley lying on his back with a hand on each pearl-handled revolver. But the handguns evidently hadn't even cleared their holsters before the train robber had died from a bullet to his neck and another that passed through an arm and his body. The house's bullet-riddled front door, like many other doors in frontier communities before it, then served as a "cooling board," on which Smalley's body was carried to the town hall, where it remained on display until witnesses to Powers' murder arrived and made positive identification. Seeing the body, an out-of-town lawman remarked, "That beats a jury trial by a long way." And the doctor who conducted a brief post mortem overlooked the obvious, calling the corpse a "splendid specimen of physical manhood."

The door never made it back to the Brown house. It was given to a Grand Rapids museum, and the whiskered train robber's two revolvers ended up being displayed for years in the window of a Grand Rapids jewelry store.

At the time of Smalley's death, authorities didn't know of his log cabin hideout, and they never recovered any of the money from his countless robberies. If Cora had any of the loot, she never let on and cried pauper when it came time to bury Smalley. She did reluctantly pay for her husband's funeral but refused to ante up the money for a headstone. And so Michigan's greatest train robber lies in an unmarked grave in McBain.

DAN HEFFRON

The Crook Who Left a Jury Hanging

Carrie Nation, who preached abstinence from alcohol and delighted in axing saloons into kindling, would have loved the Chicago Lumber Company. When the firm founded Manistique in the 1870s, it set out to ensure the little mill town would forever remain quiet, sedate, and above all, temperate. Lake Michigan wet the town's southern edge and the Manistique River flowed through its heart, bearing the community's economic well-being on its back, but the lumber company meant Manistique to be drier than Death Valley. The town grew very thirsty, and the first man able to open a saloon and pop the bung on a barrel of beer was sure to be rich. Dan Heffron wanted to be that man.

The Chicago Lumber Company made every effort to bar the likes of Dan Heffron and other saloonkeepers when it purchased land and platted the town. The company simply refused to sell or lease property for saloons. And to make sure the town stayed parched, deeds to all city lots stipulated "that said premises shall never be used by the party of the second part, its successors or assigns for the business of manufacturing, storing, or selling intoxicating liquors."

But if the company executives congratulated themselves on erecting a chained and padlocked legal fence that kept liquor and saloons from sullying their fair city, the celebration was short-lived. The company was shocked to discover that the employee who had handled the land purchase hadn't noticed or had not thought it important to mention the fact that Alex Richards held a prior claim, an original deed to a small piece of property within the proposed company town. To make matters worse, the deed carried no restrictions, and the parcel — a triangular piece of land that became known as the Flatiron Block — bounded two streets crowded with thirsty men when the town's sawmills changed shifts.

Dan Heffron arrived, determined to wet the whistle of those hard-working, lumber-company employees. Heffron had worked as a lumber-jack in the Saginaw area before moving north to speculate on property in Cheboygan, where he made enough money to open a hotel and bar. When Heffron heard that a lumber company was carving Manistique out of virgin forest along the Manistique River, the saloonkeeper sold his businesses, packed up, and again headed north.

If Heffron saw Manistique as his main chance to make it big in a small community, making more money as the town grew, he hardly blinked when told of Manistique's prohibition on booze. Within days of his arrival, Heffron learned of Richards' restriction-free property, bought a lot, and quickly nailed together a saloon. Heffron's watering hole quickly became the most popular spot in town, and above the bar he built a club, where boxing and gambling were the most conspicuous diversions. A stable of prostitutes also probably worked out of the club, but at first they maintained a low profile. Later, Heffron bought another lot on the block and opened a livery stable.

The lumber company kept a keen eye on Heffron and his saloon, hoping to shut him down when and if the barkeep tripped over any city ordinance. But Heffron skillfully tiptoed around local laws and also hid some of his illegal transgressions from authorities. On the several occasions he was charged with operating a house of prostitution, he simply applied cash when and where needed to buy his way out. And if and when that failed, he tampered with juries and "persuaded" prosecution witnesses to not appear. Also, many powerful community leaders quietly supported Heffron, and it was rumored that a local newspaper kowtowed to him in return for financial favors.

The resulting bottom line was that many California gold mines didn't make the money Heffron panned from the pockets of the alcohol-starved men who stepped up to his establishment in the Flatiron Block.

With Dan's success, more entrepreneurs flocked to Richards' triangular oasis. Seven saloons soon spilled foam on the Flatiron Block, and after the lumber company recognized the inevitable and gave up trying to keep the town dry, 29 bars plied their trade in a community of 3,000 well-oiled customers.

With the law and lumber company apparently beaten and relaxing their grip on Manistique, Heffron's ego outgrew whatever common sense he possessed. He concluded he was above the law, and he began to feel near-invincible when his brother Dennis was elected Sheriff of Schoolcraft County.

Dan Heffron may have been justified in believing he kept the well-trained town on a short leash, but he nevertheless maintained a low profile and rarely walked the dog. He never flashed his money or flouted his power, and he was as conservative in speech and manner as an undertaker. The man's distinguished silver-gray hair led to the moniker "The Silver King." When Dan walked down the street it was nearly impossible to imagine that there went a barkeep and a whoremaster.

Dan began experiencing problems, however, when he failed to catch even a wisp of his community's changing sentiment. His power base slowly eroded as Manistique matured and its citizens concluded they could no longer tolerate prostitution. Dan became as welcome in Manistique as a tourist on a budget is today in Harbor Springs. In March 1892, when Heffron was once again charged with keeping a "house of ill-fame," initially he probably wasn't too concerned. He simply did what he always did when faced with the law — he reached for cash. And when a hefty pile of greenbacks didn't squelch the charge, Dan still saw no reason to panic. From previous experience, he considered himself an artist at jury tampering and intimidating potential witnesses.

However, Heffron finally realized the gravity of his predicament when some of Manistique's leading citizens — obviously holding the county attorney in low regard — petitioned the governor to appoint Michigan's Attorney General as the prosecutor. When the governor agreed, the community whipped itself into a lather of anticipation.

They weren't disappointed. The several-day-long trial was the most exciting thing to hit Manistique since Heffron opened his bar. The curious arrived at the courthouse two hours early in hopes of getting a seat. The Manistique *Tri-Weekly Pioneer* proclaimed the trial was "exciting from the very outset" but found it stunning that "this outrage had gone on for more than twelve years." The paper's next issue declared, "Whenever you see two or three men talking together that is the matter being discussed."

Testimony was sensational and, according to the *Tri-Weekly Pioneer*, unfit for publication. But the paper went on to report that witnesses left no doubt Heffron's establishment was a "vile resort for fast men." Striving for accuracy without offending delicate Victorian sensibilities forced the editor to tap dance around the facts with the skill of Gene Kelly. The paper reported that "some witnesses had the most positive knowledge of the character of the house, had been there and taken part in the business usually carried on in such places, and this they swore to."

The defense flailed away at the prosecution and its witnesses but with no great effect. When Heffron's witnesses testified, the *Tri-Weekly* thought they actually helped the prosecution. And the defense really peed in its own boot when it called Dan Heffron to the stand where, under grueling cross-examination, he as much as convicted himself. In summation, the highly paid defense attorney strove mightily to overcome a mountain of evidence, but it was as near futile as trying to paddle a canoe up Tahquamenon Falls.

There seemed little doubt in anyone's mind what verdict the jury would return with as it filed out of the courtroom to begin deliberations. The attorneys, Heffron, and the courthouse crowd variously wandered the village streets, met at saloons to discuss the case, or went in search of food. But before a hungry man could bring a fork to his mouth, word went out that the jury had reached a decision. Heffron was sent for and was returning on foot to the courthouse when onlookers spotted a horse-drawn sleigh flying down the snow-covered street toward the defendant. As it whipped past Heffron he threw himself into the sleigh and dived under a buffalo robe while the driver lashed the horse out of town.

The police organized a pursuit and used both telegraph and telephone to cast a wide net for the fugitive. But Heffron eluded capture and made it to Delta Junction, west of Manistique, where he boarded a westbound freight. "The Silver King" was never caught, and some claim he later opened a saloon in Chicago.

But meanwhile, back in Manistique! While Heffron, as sure of the verdict as anyone, fled justice and the town, the jury remained sequestered. While the town went mildly crazy over the daring getaway, the 12 men were forgotten and good as locked up in the deliberation room. Finally, the judge ordered the jury brought in, and a less-than-surprising and very anti-climactic guilty verdict was read into the court record. More than an hour after Heffron had secured his own freedom, the jury was excused and freed to go home.

ALBERT MOLITOR

King of Presque Isle

R uling came naturally to Albert Molitor; it was in his blood — literally. As the illegitimate son of King William of Wurtemberg, Albert couldn't succeed his father, so instead he created his own kingdom half a world away from the German state where he was born. And once he assumed the mantle of leadership, Molitor proved to be a real bastard.

The future King of Presque Isle received a military-school education in his homeland and, after graduating with an engineering degree, took a position as a draftsmen in Wurtemberg's War Department. Molitor lost his job and nearly his life, however, when superiors caught him copying plans of Wurtemberg's great fortress of Uhlan and also discovered evidence Molitor was to get cash for the documents from Austria.

Rather than face a hangman's noose, Molitor — likely with royal assistance — fled to America. He stepped ashore in New York in time to join the Union Army and fight for his newly adopted country. Though he arrived in America with a badly blemished record, his service as an officer with the Army of the Potomac was exemplary.

With the defeat of the Confederacy, the newly discharged soldier relocated to Detroit, where he married, fathered a son, and took a job with the Department of Lake Survey. The young man worked closely with William E. Rogers, the department's director, and when they found a sizeable stand of virgin timber while surveying Presque Isle County in 1869, they formed the Molitor-Rogers Company to exploit their discovery. They hired Frederick Denny Larkin as a company agent and sent him to Lansing to buy the timber-rich land. As soon as Larkin consummated the purchase and returned to Detroit with the documents, Albert put pen to paper and platted the future site of Rogers City.

In 1869 Larkin recruited a boatload of Polish and German settlers and shipped them north to turn Molitor's paper city into reality. The pioneers arrived to find Molitor had laid out the village on swampy, timbered land that had to be cleared and drained. The newcomers also built a sawmill, a store, a smithy, and a boarding house, all owned by the company, not by the men who'd built the little settlement in the wilderness.

The side-wheeler *Marine City* made weekly runs between Rogers City and Detroit, and for people and supplies it was the only way into or out of the community. But the boat only operated from April to November. During the winter months the town received no supplies, and mail arrived by dog sled from Cheboygan. The route followed the shoreline, and it took ten days to two weeks of mushing to make the round trip.

The inhabitants of the tiny settlement that defined remoteness found themselves at the mercy of the Molitor-Rogers Company. Supplies were available only through the company store and at exorbitant prices. The company was also the town's only employer and even owned all dwellings, which residents rented. Some of the settlers did homestead farms, but the soil was poor and most had to find another job to put food on the table and make the necessary improvements on the land to retain ownership. When new settlers stepped off the *Marine City* they were literally placing their lives in the hands of the Molitor-Rogers Company.

The winter of 1870-71 almost proved the town's undoing. Winter came early, stayed late, set a record for snowfall, and turned male brass monkeys into eunuchs. The *Marine City* was late delivering supplies, and by the time the boat finally arrived, the harbor was frozen over. The *Marine City* managed to dock a few miles away at Hammond's Bay, and all barrels, sacks, boxes, and other cargo had to be lugged by hand back to Rogers City. Long before spring arrived, the entire population found their daily fare reduced to an ever-dwindling quantity of boiled potatoes, bread, and a legume de jour of either dried beans or peas that had had everything but indigestion cooked out of them.

The *Marine City* arrived again in April to great rejoicing, especially by William E. Rogers, who had had enough. Holding to the hunger-etched opinion that this was no way to make money or build an empire, he said goodbye to Rogers City, the State of Michigan, and the whole damned

Midwest and returned to the East Coast where winters were more civilized.

Rogers' departure left Molitor in complete control of the city, and he quickly moved to strengthen his settlement and extend his authority over the entire county. First, Rogers City needed more settlers, so in German-language newspapers in Detroit and Cleveland Molitor placed an ad that read, "Men Wanted — Carpenters and other workmen in the sawmill and woods to fell trees. There is also opportunity to obtain good government and state land near Rogers City. Work and home seekers should come Monday with the steamer *Marine City* directly to Rogers City — Albert Molitor." The ad helped boost the population, which in turn put more money into Molitor's pocket and more votes into his ballot box.

The last obstacle in Molitor's road to county control was the Crawford family, who had arrived in Presque Isle County a few years before the Molitor-Rogers Company had come into existence. Headed by patriarch Francis, the Crawfords settled north of Rogers City, platted a town called Crawford's Quarry, and attracted a few settlers. The family's three sons cut cordwood, which they sold as fuel to passing steamers.

In 1873 or '74 one of the sons won election to a high county office (which son, which office, and the exact year differ, depending on the source), which sparked a tug of war between Molitor's Rogers City and the Crawfords' little settlement for political control of the county. Crawford's Quarry built a courthouse and declared itself the county seat. Not to be outdone, Molitor named Rogers City the county seat, put forward his own slate of trained-to-the-leash county-office candidates for election, and then ensured their victory. On election day, Molitor presented voters with two different-colored ballots, a red ballot that contained his hand-picked slate of office seekers and a white ballot that listed independent or Crawford-backed candidates. Molitor positioned himself next to the Rogers City polling booth and made sure only red papers went into the ballot box.

Immediately following his candidates' landslide victories, the empowered Molitor ordered the formerly elected Crawford son to hand over all county records. When the man refused, Molitor sent his newly elected sheriff to retrieve the records and arrest him. The sheriff got his hands on the county records, but Crawford had lit out of town, jumped a passing ship, and disappeared — forever.

But that didn't stop the dispute over the location of the county seat. Each town built a courthouse and burned their rival's, repeating the cycle at least twice — early Presque Isle County's version of a torch-passing ceremony. In 1875 Albert Molitor had himself elected county treasurer and permanently extinguished Crawford's Quarry's hope of landing the county seat.

Upon assuming the office of county treasurer, Molitor even further consolidated his political and economic control. In fact in all but title, he ruled Presque Isle County like a king. And except for a crown, Albert Molitor looked the part. A photograph from the era reveals a man of obvious confidence and swagger. He stood over six feet tall, had an honest face anchored by a square jaw and a chest that thrust out to meet the world or push it aside if it got in his way. There was a forthrightness about the man in the photograph, and none of the meanness that he soon visited upon his subjects.

The newly elected Treasurer of Presque Isle County not only lusted for power, but also after women. Before moving north, he divorced his Detroit wife, and any woman in Rogers City he took a sexual interest in, he raped. Most times, the County Treasurer would simply walk into a house and order a woman off to bed. If she refused, resisted or complained afterwards, her husband lost his job and they lost their company house. Women either put up and shut up or, as Molitor was fond of saying, "They could take the beach and walk out."

Molitor had proven himself a sexual predator even before he gained complete control over the county. Once, when taken with the beauty of a German woman in a photograph shown by her brother, Molitor used the man to lure his sister to Rogers City with an offer of passage and a job as Molitor's housekeeper. Upon her arrival he forced himself on her but turned the rape into seduction with a false promise of marriage. When she became pregnant in the winter of 1873, Molitor loaded her on a sleigh and drove to Detroit. Arriving in the big city, where the girl knew no one, Molitor threw his pregnant lover out onto a street corner and headed back to Rogers City. The young woman found her way to a police station, where a lawyer learned of her dire condition and subsequently brought suit against Albert Molitor in a Wayne County court. The woman was awarded a $10,000 settlement, but the papers were never served in Presque Isle County, and so the young mother never received a dime.

Albert Molitor treated the rest of his subjects no better. He continued to control who was hired and fired in Rogers City, and his company store held a monopoly on all food and merchandise. He determined the prices and even decided who was allowed to purchase food and supplies. As the county treasurer he severely raised taxes on property owned by enemies or on land he desired. When the property was forfeited to the state for non-payment of those taxes, Molitor took possession through low bids and then clear-cut timber before actually having to pay for the parcels, which he let revert again to the state.

Another of Molitor's personal fund raisers was to issue county bonds without voter approval and then essentially embezzling the funds. For instance, once under the guise of community improvement he issued $8,000 worth of bonds for the construction of a school building. When the bonds sold, he threw up a $50 building and pocketed the rest of the money. On another occasion the county issued $30,000 worth of bonds that Molitor unloaded quickly at a sharp discount and used the money as if it was his personal income. Molitor kept poor or no records of county financial transactions or bond repayment schedules, with the result that the county ultimately defaulted on all its bonds and debts.

And though Molitor may have considered himself infallible royalty, his edicts and actions didn't go totally unchallenged. As early as 1874, even as Molitor was consolidating his control, there were open signs of revolt. A group of homesteaders held secret meetings that year to plot against Molitor's tyranny, and subsequently — whether as a result of the meetings or just a spontaneous uprising — a mob stormed the company store shouting for Molitor to turn over his account books. Molitor yelled back, "Go to Hell," as he was pushed and shoved out into the street, where royal blood prevailed. He dared the mob to hang him, and when the sheriff arrived, Molitor told him to find something better to do saying, "I'll handle this mob of peasants." The angry crowd milled about and shouted threats for the rest of the day, while Molitor called them cowards and swine. When he wanted to have dinner, the crowd wouldn't let him go inside, so he set a table up in the street and had his meal served there. After a day of demands and chest pounding, the crowd finally dissolved and went home, proving nothing other than the futility of threatening Molitor.

A year passed before a more serious threat to Molitor's rule surfaced. Would-be entrepreneur Hermann Hoeft arrived in Roger City in 1873 wanting to enter the lumber business and open a store. But as a result of Molitor's continued lock on both, Hoeft's businesses never amounted to the sale of a can of beans. So in 1875 he attempted to break Molitor's monopoly by filing a lawsuit. Encouraging and supporting Hoeft's efforts was former Molitor supporter Andrew E. Banks, Judge of Probate for Presque Isle County.

In fact, the jurist soon became motivated enough to take the law into his own hands. In August 1875, not long after the lawsuit was filed, he organized a meeting of dissidents outside Rogers City, away from Molitor's prying eyes. After swearing the men to secrecy on the pain of death, the judge called for Molitor's assassination, saying, "Twelve men make a jury, and what twelve men do, everybody got to follow." That's hardly the law, but it sure was persuasive coming from a county judge. Banks adjourned the meeting and called for everyone to gather again three days later.

At the second meeting, on August 23rd, the men received firearms and each of them fortified their courage with a shot of whiskey. Also before the conspirators left on their mission, Banks gave a pair of his boots to one of them to wear. The boots made a distinctive heel mark and would be immediately identified as belonging to Banks who, while the killers rode to Rogers City, went to a friend's house to establish an alibi.

When the group reached town they walked up an alley and gathered at a window that looked into Molitor's office. The assassins drew their weapons, aimed at the window, and unleashed a storm of lead into the office. Edward Sullivan, a store clerk, absorbed a torrent of bullets and fell dead. Molitor was mortally wounded but stubbornly clung to life. He was taken to Detroit where he died on September 9, 1875.

Though Banks was immediately suspected of having a hand in the killings, his alibi was airtight. And when the distinctive heel marks from his boots turned up in the mud outside the office window, Banks claimed that, several days before the shooting, he had left the footwear at a repair shop, from where the boots had been stolen.

Local friends and supporters of Molitor asked the governor to send in the militia to keep the peace and end mob rule, but when Michigan's adjutant general visited Rogers City a few days after the shooting, he found no reason to honor the request.

After Molitor's death, his lumber mill was dismantled and the pieces and property sold. Someone else bought the company store, although not the monopoly that had gone with it. Hermann Hoeft became a political force in Presque Isle, filling another vacuum created by Molitor's death.

In spite of much finger pointing, Molitor's murder remained unsolved until 1891, when William Repke stepped forward and confessed to being a reluctant member of the gang that killed Molitor and Sullivan. Repke felt he would soon be meeting Saint Peter and wanted to do so with a clean conscience. It was left unsaid that Repke found the courage to confess at the bottom of a liquor bottle and, in fact, spilled the beans while drunk. Repke also named another ten men who took part in the shootings and was later persuaded to testify for the prosecution to further clear his conscience. Five of the men, including Repke, were convicted and sentenced to life imprisonment at Jackson State Prison in 1895. During the trials of the five, Judge Banks was clearly implicated as being at the center of the deadly conspiracy, but he escaped all criminal charges.

Once inside the foreboding prison walls, Repke had a change of heart. As reported in the *Clare Sentinel*, "Repke now makes affidavit that the evidence he gave was false. He further represents that he was induced to swear falsely at the trial upon assurance that by doing so he would free himself." He also swore in the affidavit that he was drunk at the time of the first confession. By 1901, given that prosecutors had made a monumental legal mistake by not revealing the circumstances of Repke's confession, the five convicted assassins were granted pardons, and the other five men named by Repke were never brought to trial.

Molitor's final resting place is Detroit's Elmwood Cemetery. His divorced wife lies at his side, as does their infant son, who died in 1870. Befitting the man who spent a lifetime lusting after power and women, a 30-foot-tall phallic symbol, a memorial column, stands rampant above his grave.

CUT-THROATS

JAMES CARR
"A Blood-stained and Guilty Soul"

When passing through Clare County in the early 1880s, you had to hand it to James Carr. Well, you really didn't have to, but it was easier handing it to Carr than having him take it from you, because the latter could get you an anonymous grave. Carr owned Clare County's biggest and best combination whorehouse/saloon and literally made money by the bucketful from booze and prostitutes. But never satisfied and always wanting more, he also regularly rolled drunks in his saloons, introduced white slavery to the state, and set fire to his competition. When the Clare County Prosecuting Attorney called Carr, "a blood-stained and guilty soul," he was not nominating him as the area's businessman of the year.

James Carr drew his first breath in Rochester, New York, in 1855. In 1875 he moved to Toledo, Ohio, where he lived for less than a year before drifting to Chicago. Carr arrived in the Harrison, Michigan, area in 1878 and found honest employment with lumberman Scott Gerish.

At the time, Harrison was Hell's waiting room. The town had started quietly enough, with a few raw buildings surrounded by thousands of acres of virgin white pine. But the Flint & Pere Marquette Railroad, already in Clare, was pulled like a magnet to those vast stands of timber, and when a 10-mile branch line reached Harrison, so — in wholesale quantities — did sin.

Initially, the town came close to pure anarchy. Brawls were commonplace and violent deaths unreported, and when lawmen were finally hired, they served as hardly more than window dressing. The men with the star rarely arrested anyone, because lumberjacks would rush the lawmen and liberate their brethren. When interviewed by the *Detroit News* in 1929, former Harrison resident Olivier Gosine recalled an afternoon when 27½ fights festooned Harrison's streets. He explained, "A fellow came up to me and said he could lick any man in Clare County. I told him he was taking in a lot of territory and hit him on the jaw, laying him cold as a mackerel. That was the half fight." Gosine also recalled that "jacks hated the sight of an official. I saw five officers holding revolvers in both hands, hold a crowd of 200 at bay so they could take a prisoner to jail." Gosine describes a time (probably after 1884) when there at least *was* law in Harrison. Oliver Beamer, a Harrison saloon owner during the Carr era, remembered that "there wasn't any law in those days. There were fights galore, and if anybody was killed he was taken out and buried and nothing was done about it."

In the early 1880s Harrison expanded faster than a California Gold Rush town. Amidst the new homes and shops, the railroad set aside property for a courthouse, and Harrison thought itself grand enough to become the county seat. Problem was the courthouse already lay in Farwell. There was plenty of chin wagging over moving the courthouse to Harrison, but the Farwellites weren't about to give up the building and the prestige that came with it. And then the oddest thing just happened to happen, Farwell's courthouse "mysteriously" burned to the ground. With that seat of justice in ashes, the county board of supervisors did end up budgeting money to build a courthouse in Harrison but didn't fund a jail. Now this was the kind of community where a man of low morals, and a mean streak mixed with just a soupçon of intelligence could go far.

So after three years in the woods, James Carr decided to prey on lumberjacks, rather than be one. Though the thriving village of 2,000 rough and tumble individuals already hosted 20 saloons, numerous hotels, and more than a few prostitutes, Carr built a two-story saloon and bordello on a hill overlooking the town (where the city's water tower now stands). When platting Harrison, the surveyor had not included the hill within the village's limits because he thought it too steep and rocky to be usable. So Carr's business was outside the legal jurisdiction of Harrison, and it literally became the town's high point and the bull's eye for every man aiming for low women and strong liquor.

Carr's two-story "Devil's Ranch Stockade" was a beacon for depravity. Each night 50 to 250 men raised hell in the rough-framed building and so-called hotel. They danced to music from a beat-up piano and raised so many glasses of beer and liquor you would have thought that swinging an axe all day was simply a way to stay in shape for a night of hoisting drinks. So much money was thrown at bartenders that the saloon dispensed with cash registers. Bartenders simply crammed money into pails lining the back of the bar, and when a container started to overflow they took it to Carr's office for counting. When a customer passed out from too much 40-rod whiskey (a nasty concoction of tobacco, cheap whiskey, hot peppers, and damn near anything else at hand, of which it was said you couldn't drink a shot and walk 40 rods without falling down) the saloon's bouncers dragged the drunk to a back room, turned his pockets inside out, and confiscated anything of value before pitching the hapless jack out the back door.

If not enough men were drinking themselves senseless, the bartenders laced drinks with knockout drops, and the bouncers waited for the lumberjacks to pitch over like felled trees. Many never recovered from the spiked drinks says Olivier Gosine, who worked a short while for Carr and later served as a sexton for the Harrison cemetery, adding that he personally buried more than one of the saloon's victims. In fact so many lives ended at the Devil's Ranch Stockade, the hill on which it stood became known as Deadman's Hill.

The ranch became a huge, efficient smelting machine that separated lumberjacks from their money. When one of Carr's dancing girls took the floor, it was as if the sky rained money and the saloon's roof leaked. A big tin pail was placed in the middle of the dance floor, and the women's clothes came off as money poured into it. And the strippers were sure not to peel off the last layers until the pail overflowed and spilled money onto the floor.

The buying of "time tickets" proved to be another almost effortless way for Carr to make money. Most lumber companies didn't pay their crews until logs reached the sawmills. When a lumberjack wanted an advance against his earnings, the camp foreman issued him a time ticket — a piece of paper saying the company owed the bearer X amount of money. The tickets could be redeemed for real money at company headquarters downstate, so many local businessmen treated the tickets the same as cash.

Not Carr. He accepted time tickets at only 50% of face value and of course redeemed them later at full value.

Carr also procured prostitutes in his own unique way. "Stockade" in the bordello's name accurately described the place. A wooden wall literally surrounded Devil's Ranch and wasn't there to keep customers out, but to keep the working women in. Just because it's the world's oldest profession didn't mean recruitment came easy. There was no "be all you can be" slogan extolling the virtues of prostitution, then or now.

When Carr came up short of whores he became proactive. Kidnapping a young woman off the streets of Saginaw or Bay City proved the most direct and expeditious method of recruitment. Carr also advertised in downstate papers for chambermaids and waitresses for his Harrison hotel. When a new employee arrived at the Harrison depot she was met by a Carr associate — probably Maggie Duncan, Carr's lover and whorehouse matron — taken to the Devil's Ranch, and roughly introduced to her new world. More often than not, these young women simply disappeared, never to be heard from again.

And working for the Devil couldn't have been any worse than working for Carr. He used prostitutes hard. Many of the young women were kept as virtual slaves, and for those who crossed him or, in his opinion, didn't work hard enough, he slipped on his brass knuckles and personally administered savage beatings.

Jennie King was one of the few known to have who escaped. King answered a newspaper ad, expecting to work in Carr's Harrison "hotel." Shortly after her introduction to stockade life, she fled, only to be caught and beaten. Undeterred, the brave and desperate woman escaped again the same night, wearing only a nightgown, and reached a house in Harrison where she knocked and gained sanctuary. Within minutes, Maggie Duncan knocked on the door and demanded the family give Jennie up. With the terrified young woman hiding under a bed, the family refused and instead arranged to have a Midland Deputy Sheriff take their unexpected visitor to Midland.

Maggie Duncan, herself, had turned tricks out of a track-side shack near Farwell until Carr happened across her. When the two met, love bloomed, or something did because Maggie and Jim fit together like a lock and key. She continued on her career track, but moved up to management and ran the whorehouse side of the Harrison ranch. The only appreciable period when the two were apart, including after death, was when one or the other were behind bars. Maggie and Jim never formalized their relationship with vows, rings or such, but it does appear there may be a true love story here. It's just buried under a mountain of sin, degradation, greed, cruelty, and exploitive sex. At the least, it has the makings of a great country and western ballad.

Within months of its opening, the whorehouse and saloon on Deadman's Hill made Carr a wealthy and locally powerful man. In 1883 the *Clare Press* reported "that Jim Carr, the proprietor of Harrison's bawdyhouse, has already cleared $20,000 from his business and has his stake set at double that amount." At his height of power, Carr was above the law and could get away with darn near anything. Part of the reason rested in the fact that Clare County Sheriff John Cramer had his hand permanently attached to Carr's billfold. When Cramer ran for re-election in 1884, an outraged *Clare Press* editorial said in part, "John Cramer, who is on the stump for sheriff, deserves the support of thugs, thieves, pimps, and bums and will probably get their votes. He doesn't deserve the vote of a decent man." Another editorial shouted, "Thieves are running Cramer again for Sheriff ... (because they) know whom they can depend on for protection in their crimes."

But just owning the law, of and by itself, didn't allow Carr to act with impunity. Many influential people in Clare County and northern Michigan accepted wild living, bad liquor, and whorehouses as just a natural part of the frontier landscape. An 1884 editorial in the Harrison *Cleaver and Standard* declared, "Saloons and illicit houses are a necessity in a new country."

Carr had the law on his side and benefited from a laissez-faire attitude from a large segment of polite society. Plus most importantly, he was meaner than an abscessed tooth. Few people crossed him, and those who did were either drunk or had misplaced their instinct for self-preservation.

Ike Jacobs, a pretty tough man in his own right, was one of the luckier men to go up against Carr. He lived — barely — to tell about it. One night Jacobs washed into Carr's saloon on a wave of alcohol that left him high and dry at the bar rail. He ordered and quickly downed one round, then hammered the bar demanding a second. Jacobs was known as a hellishly mean drunk, and so the bartender refused to refloat him with a second round. Jacobs called down hellfire and damnation on the barkeep and demanded to see Carr, who had already heard the ruckus and was on the way from his office. After an exchange of barroom pleasantries, Carr slipped on a pair of brass knuckles, walked out from behind the bar, and sucker-punched Jacobs. Ike went down hard, and Carr went to work kicking him repeatedly about the head. When Carr tired of beating Ike, two lumberjacks dragged the unconscious and badly injured troublemaker outdoors and dumped him into his wagon. They untied Ike's horse from the hitching post and gave it a pat on the flank trusting it would find its way home. Jacob wore the scars of his encounter with Carr for the rest of his life, including the loss of sight in one eye. The law, on the other hand, never blinked an eye.

Perhaps it was just his reputation, but many people who knew Carr swore an aura of danger and violence surrounded the six-foot tall, soft-spoken man with deep-set eyes. Always well-groomed and gentlemanly in appearance, the only thing hinting at a wild side was a brushy mustache that hid his upper lip and the ends of which were long enough to blow in the wind. Carr couldn't walk down a street or take a train ride without being noticed and talked about. In short he'd become famous, but the tide of public opinion would soon shift and he'd become infamous. But not before he established another saloon and bawdyhouse, this one in Meredith.

After the railroad chugged into Harrison in 1880, a branch line began snaking toward Meredith, a one-log-cabin village 10 miles to the north. When the railroad reached Meredith, the berg briefly became a northern Michigan boomtown. Forty buildings crowded streets so new they still sprouted stumps. Overnight the town found itself with a drug store, hotel, blacksmith shop, post office, saloons, and a bawdyhouse. Thomas McClennon platted the town and built the Corrigan House, in which he installed a bar reputedly long enough to hold 100 lumberjacks. McClennon didn't sell lots in town, he rented them, and if the renter wanted to open a saloon he had to ante up another $400 on top of the regular $300 annual rent.

The coming of the railroad also made it possible to finally lumber the Meredith area, whose stands of white pine had previously escaped the axe because of the lack of streams big enough to float the logs to the mills. Fifty lumber companies sent a veritable army into the woods — with some camps employing 2,000 men — in a final assault on the timber yards of Clare County.

And there sat Meredith in the middle of it all, serving as the supply depot for the lumber companies and an oasis of booze and loose women for the lumberjacks. No wonder Carr looked at Meredith and saw potentially huge profits for another Devil's Ranch. And besides, it was the kind of place that when a bartender once asked a customer to pay for the beer he just drank, the bartender was shot and killed because the customer didn't consider the beer worth 10 cents. Yes, Meredith teemed with the kind of verdant lawlessness in which Carr could put down roots and bloom.

But before Carr opened for business in Meredith, in late 1883 or early 1884, he first eliminated his competition. Peter McCarthy already operated a whorehouse in Meredith, and Carr simply told him to pack up and get out. When McCarthy ignored the directive, an unknown assailant beat him to death with a billiard stick. With McCarthy out of the way, Carr built a second Devil's Ranch Stockade on 40 acres adjoining the village of Meredith. With Maggie Duncan still running the Harrison operation, Belle Baker oversaw the prostitution side of the business for Carr and ran a crew composed of Daisy Young, Frankie Osborne, Edith Stowell and Mae Harvey. Some claimed the women weren't much to look at, when in fact, some of them were simply too much to look at. One man recalled the women were so wide they "had to go through doors sideways," which may account for Carr once again trying to lure young women to his bawdyhouse with false ads in downstate newspapers.

By summer 1884, with ranches in both Meredith and Harrison, Carr's power peaked, and his career began a long, downhill slide. Carr just didn't know it. Occasionally, he would commit a crime that simply couldn't be overlooked, and he'd be arrested, charged, and then let go. And when Frankie Osborne, a crowd-favorite dancer/stripper, was beaten to death in the Meredith ranch on June 15, 1884, it looked like her killing wouldn't even warrant that bit of legal sham.

Jim Carr

Maggie Carr

Carr immediately topped the suspect list. It was common knowledge he operated with a short fuse attached to an explosive temper, and people just took it for granted that Frankie happened to be within killing distance when Carr detonated. Plus Carr had a record for beating prostitutes. Just the previous year he had been arrested for assaulting another Meredith employee. The charge in part read, "James Carr, with force and arms, in the township of Franklin, Clare County, in and upon Edith Stowell alias 'Edith Wallace,' said James Carr, in his right hand, then and there held a cane or club, did make assault with intent to do great bodily harm on the above named person." Sources disagree over whether charges were dropped, or Carr spent a few days in jail. Whichever, it evidently had little rehabilitative effect, because rumors continued to circulate that Carr regularly used brass knuckles on his prostitutes.

Still, the murder of Frankie Osborne passed all but unnoticed in Clare County's law-enforcement community, and it appeared as if the young woman's brutal death didn't raise a blip on the town's moribund conscience.

If the law turned its back on Carr, Clare County newspapers did not. D. E. Alward, editor of the *Clare Press* demanded reform, as did the editor of the Farwell paper. Alward wrote that Sheriff Cramer was a "free man only because he has not received his just deserts." Both newspapers taunted Cramer and dared the sheriff to take them to court for libel.

Clare County citizens also finally had their fill of rampant lawlessness, and a pair of reform candidates came forward to run for sheriff and county prosecutor. Carr spread the word that anyone who supported the reformers flirted with danger, but both reform candidates won election. Carr should have seen the writing on the wall; instead he worried about his competition.

Carr's two saloons and bawdyhouses brought him a small fortune every night, and still he was obsessive about not sharing his drink- and sex-starved clientele with anyone else. When James Silkworth opened a whorehouse and bar just four miles away at Arnold Lake, Carr mentally counted and recounted the money the damned upstart might be siphoning from his pockets. That the sheriff who had protected him for years had just been voted out of office, and a D.A. sworn to cleaning up the county had just been swept into office never even entered Carr's mind when he decided to get Silkworth.

On December 1, 1884, Carr met with Sammy Johns and John Ryan in Meredith's swankest saloon, the Corrigan House. Sammy and John were never above doing something against the law for the right amount of money. So when Carr waved $250 in front of the two as proposed payment for burning down Silkworth's place, they struck a deal. Carr should have checked to see if either could strike a match. The plan called for the pair to burn Silkworth's while Carr showed himself in Harrison and solidified an alibi. On the agreed-upon night, Sammy and John arrived at the Arnold Lake whorehouse only to discover they were both incinerationally challenged. They splashed oil on the building but simply couldn't get the fuel or the wood siding to ignite. After several pathetic attempts, they put their matches away and headed home.

Several days later, Carr returned to Meredith and found Silkworth's place not only standing but without even a visible scorch mark. Sammy and John, knowing they were flirting with serious injury, anxiously met with Carr and tried to explain the fire-retardant qualities of dry wood. Carr ordered the two to meet him near Arnold Lake that night. Loaded with oil, pistols, and matches they snuck up to the back wall of the whorehouse, piled shavings and kindling next to the wall, doused the stuff with oil, and lit a match. Whoompf. Carr and his henchmen stayed hidden and enjoyed watching naked customers and working girls run from Silkworth's front door.

The next day it would have been near impossible to find a person in Clare County who didn't believe Carr either set the fire or hired it done.

Less than a month later, on January 1, 1885, the new sheriff and prosecuting attorney W.A. Burritt took office and announced the construction of a jail would begin immediately and that Frankie Osborne's death and the torching of Silkworth's business would receive their attention in the near future.

In March a grand jury convened to look into Osborne's death. The next day, Carr appeared in court and was charged with her murder. Carr scoffed at the charge and, while putting on his hat and gloves, asked in a voice dripping with scorn, how much money it would take to make the case go away. Judge Henry Hart, in no mood for insults, ordered Carr to uncover his head and then sent him to jail without setting bail. The sheriff also rounded up seven of Carr's prostitutes in Meredith and Harrison and charged them with being disorderly persons.

Jim Carr's trial for the murder of Frankie Osborne began in Harrison on May 12, 1885. Daisy Young, a prostitute who claimed to have seen Carr beating Frankie on the night she died, was the prosecution's star witness. Daisy testified Carr struck Frankie, knocked her down, kicked and stomped her, then lifted the victim by the hair and again kicked her. When Carr tired of beating Frankie, Daisy added, he turned to Murphy, the bouncer, and told him, "Now, God damn her, you finish her." Daisy said that after Murphy's beating, Frankie was unable to rise but managed to drag herself to a bench, from where two women helped Frankie to her room.

Carr's highly paid lawyers from Flint and Saginaw punched numerous holes in Daisy's testimony. Dr. Scott then took the stand as a defense witness and said that if Carr had hit Frankie, the deceased told him that it was Murphy's beating that sent her to bed. Scott also testified that when he attended Frankie on the night of her death, he at first suspected malaria because of her high fever. It was only after Murphy admitted to beating the girl that Scott opened her robe and saw the many bruises covering Frankie's body. Murphy, by the way, couldn't testify, as he had died two months before the trial. Lewis Schramm, a musician who worked in Carr's Meredith saloon, then took the stand and swore he saw Murphy beat Frankie two days before she died. He testified that Murphy knocked her to the floor, beat her, and then made her dance. Schramm said she collapsed into bed after the beating and died there two days later.

Carr opened his billfold to anyone who would testify that Murphy did the killing, telling one man, "You can not hurt a dead man, why not lay the murder of Frankie on Murphy?" Carr's attorneys ended their defense by calling the long line of paid witnesses, who spread confusion and defamed Daisy Young. Even the prosecutor, in closing, called Daisy a "prostituted wreck" but claimed, "Her evidence stands unimpeached." After four hours of deliberation, the jury reported that it was hung, with three for acquittal and nine voting guilty. Judge Henry Hart dismissed the jury, ordered a new trial to start in December, and changed the venue to Gratiot County.

But before Carr could get one legal monkey off his back, another climbed on board. In October he was arrested and charged with burning down Silkworth's whorehouse the previous December. Carr paid a $5,000 bond and walked, but you can't help but think he finally realized that Prosecutor Burritt was the equivalent of a legal snapping turtle that, having sunk his teeth into Jim, wasn't about to let go.

Carr's second trial for Frankie's murder got under way on December 15th, with Daisy once again describing the beating Frankie took at the hands of Carr and the orders he gave Murphy to continue. The defense called many of the same witnesses as in the first trial to again discredit Daisy. Jim Carr then took the stand and said he wasn't even in Meredith the night Frankie died; he was ill and bedridden in Harrison. He testified that when he heard about Frankie's death, he sent John Dewey to an undertaker with orders to buy a casket and ship it to Meredith. Carr wanted dear Frankie returned to Harrison in the casket for burial. Carr also claimed that when he found out Murphy had beaten Frankie to death, he fired him. Murphy, of course, remained conveniently dead and unable to rebut the story. Furthermore, Carr claimed that Daisy Young wasn't at the Meredith ranch the night Osborne died. John Dewey then took the stand and vouched for Carr being sick in Harrison the night of Frankie's death.

But somehow the prosecution subsequently got to Dewey, because he retook the witness stand and recanted his earlier testimony. Yes, Carr was in Meredith the night Frankie died. Yes, Carr asked him to perjure himself for money. Yes, Carr paid him to point the finger at Murphy. In short, the second trial got as messy and confusing as the first.

On Christmas Eve the jury retired to deliberate and on Christmas Day filed back into the courtroom and pronounced Jim Carr guilty of manslaughter. The judge sentenced Carr to 15 years in Jackson State Prison. Carr's lawyers requested a new trial, which the judge denied. Carr was taken to Jackson on January 22, 1886, while his high-paid lawyers spent more of his money working on appeals.

With Carr in prison making shoes, the law turned to Maggie. In April 1886 she sat in a Clare County courtroom and heard a jury find her guilty of keeping a house of prostitution. The conviction won Maggie a one-year, all-expenses-paid stay in the Detroit House of Correction. Upon her arrival at the prison and during the routine search all incoming prisoners undergo, guards discovered $1,500 stuffed inside the tops of Maggie's stockings.

After spending large sums of Carr's dwindling funds, his lawyers appealed his conviction to the Supreme Court of Michigan. After due deliberation the court found Carr "a very depraved man" but ruled his conviction and sentencing was unfairly based on inconclusive evidence and ordered a new trial. Prosecutor Burritt dropped the murder charges, but didn't give up. The day Carr walked out of prison, the sheriff rearrested him for arson. It cost him $5,000 to post a bond and walk free. Carr returned to Harrison, where Maggie joined him a month later after serving her time. But before they could draw a breath and make a dime, the sheriff raided the Harrison stockade and took six prostitutes into custody. They weren't released until Carr dug deep into his wallet and paid their fines.

With their empire crumbling and all but broke, Carr and Maggie moved to Meredith and continued to do the only thing they knew how to — run a house of prostitution. But the law gave them no respite. On August 30, 1887, the sheriff raided the Meredith stockade and arrested two women, Carr, and a handful of customers. Maggie, however, escaped after drawing a gun on a cop. The two women pleaded guilty and were told to leave the county or go to jail. They left. Carr found himself indicted for operating a house of prostitution and without enough money to make bail. God knows where, but he found friends to bail him out.

Carr may have been thick-headed, but he finally realized the law in Clare County couldn't be called off and wouldn't give up. The Meredith stockade sat on the Clare and Gladwin County line, and Carr came up with a scheme that must have made him feel as clever as Wile E. Coyote. But sadly for Carr, his efforts proved as successful as the can't-buy-a-break cartoon character's. A short, jaw-dropping story in the *Clare Press* on September 30th reported, "Carr's notorious Devil's Ranch at Meredith has been closed and moved a few rods into Gladwin County to avoid prosecution." The bawdyhouse was dragged — lock, stock, and barrel — across the county line and opened under a new name, "The State Road Hotel."

The citizens of Gladwin County, however, didn't send the Welcome Wagon. In an act of purification only a week after the move, vigilantes raided Carr's den of iniquity and burned it to the ground. That same day the *Clare Press* reported that "twenty so-called 'respectable citizens' of Meredith have petitioned in favor of a house of prostitution in their midst."

On November 15, 1887, Carr found himself once more in Prosecuting Attorney Burritt's crosshairs when his trial for burning the Silkworth place convened. But what at first looked like a can't-lose case quickly fell apart. The prosecutor's chief witness, Sammy Jones, confessed to helping Carr torch Silkworth's business, but John Ryan, the other arsonist and collaborating witness, had escaped from jail and vanished. Since Jones was a confessed criminal, his testimony was leavened with doubt. The jury brought back a quick not-guilty verdict.

Carr walked free from the arson charges, but four years of trials, appeals, and the law constantly nipping at his heels had left him penniless and a physical wreck. Both the Meredith and Harrison stockades lay in ruins, and he and Maggie both suffered from alcoholism and venereal disease. It was as if the venom they had inflicted on others over the years had come back to poison them. But on the bright side, the dawn of 1888 marked the first time in three years Carr's name failed to appear on a court docket. Maggie and her man lived a quiet life. He drank. She drank and turned tricks to keep them in alcohol.

As the 1880s drew to a close, Clare County was without white pine or lumberjacks. Meredith had all but dried up and blown away, with only a few residents keeping it from becoming a ghost town. Maggie earned enough money at her old trade to barely keep the couple in food and booze, and by 1892 the pair were reduced to living in an old railroad shed south of Meredith. The previous winter had been hard on them, and both were sick. An ex-logging-camp cook named Lame Bob volunteered to nurse the couple and make sure they took their medicine, but more often than not he fell into a drunken stupor.

On March 21st, or the 12th (depending on the source), 1892, a doctor along with a justice of the peace arrived at the trackside shack to check on Jim and Maggie. Lame Bob was dead drunk and had let the fire in the stove die out. Jim Carr, at 37-years-old, lay dead on a straw pallet, and

Maggie was within a breath or two of life's great abyss. The doctor ordered the J.P. to rebuild the fire, hoping the warmth might revive Maggie, but she died within hours, racing to catch up with her life's one great love. (Some sources claim Maggie recovered enough to be moved to the county poorhouse where she died a few months later, but most sources conclude she died the same day as Jim and several sources speak of their joint burial.)

The obituary notices and personal testimonials for Carr were extraordinary in their bluntness. The Clare *Democrat and Press* said he was the "proprietor of one of the dirtiest dens that ever robbed manhood of its beauty or steeped in sins the souls of women. ... Evil so predominated their general make-up, that all that was good sank from sight." The Gladwin *County Record* obituary notice read, in part, "James Carr, known throughout the state, and especially northern Michigan as one of the most notorious and wicked of its inhabitants, died in a log camp near Meredith Tuesday morning, unwept, unhonored and unsung by all save his wife, Maggie who remained faithfully by his side. . ... For a long time (he) kept a 'stockade ranch' near the village of Harrison, a resort of the vilest character. Herein it was asserted, the worst forces of evil were practiced and the inmates were prisoners, subjected to the grossest cruelty and outrages. ... The county will probably have to assist at his funeral." But a man who knew Carr probably summed up Carr's life best, "You could say almost anything about him. Because no matter how bad it was, it was probably true."

Legend has it that seven preachers refused to officiate at the Carrs' interment. Finally a gang of old lumberjacks took the funeral into their own hands and carried Jim and Maggie to the Meredith cemetery, where one of the men read a few passages from a bible. The couple was then set six feet under, a few feet outside the cemetery's boundary. Jim and Maggie were too wicked to be accorded sacred ground.

STEPHEN G. SIMMONS

Michigan's Dr. Jekyll and Mr. Hyde

When Stephen G. Simmons rode into the Michigan Territory with a wave of immigrants from western New York in 1824 or '25, little did anyone suspect the man could have easily provided Robert Louis Stevenson with all the inspiration he needed for writing *The Strange Case of Dr. Jekyll and Mr. Hyde*, or that his dual personality would lead to a killing, an execution, and a national-first legal milestone.

Soon after arriving in Michigan, Simmons built a tavern on the banks of the lower branch of the Rouge River roughly 15 miles west of Detroit on the Detroit-Chicago Road (present-day US-12). Standing over six feet tall and weighing more than 250 pounds, the tavern owner stood out in a crowd. He was a virtual Goliath who outweighed the average man of the 1820s by almost 100 pounds, and surprisingly, once you got past his size, he seemed both refined and of noble bearing. People thought him a man of culture and education and an obvious asset to the rough-edged Michigan frontier. Adding to the initial good impression, Simmons appeared to care deeply for his frail and chronically ill wife, and also impressed his new neighbors as a model father to his two daughters.

But it didn't take long for the bloom to wear off the welcome extended to Simmons.

Behind closed doors Simmons subjected his wife and daughters to a life of fulminating terror in which loving father or husband could, in the blink of an eye, turn into a 250-pound hellhound bent on inflicting pain and suffering. The catalyst that transformed the gentlemanly behemoth into vicious ghoul was alcohol. A couple of shots of whiskey and Dr. Jekyll disappeared and Mr. Hyde took his place.

The community, too, grew to fear and hate the outwardly refined Simmons, and neighbors quickly learned to steer well clear of the man when he drank. But that was not always possible. When under the influence, Simmons searched out victims, picked fights, and inflicted painful beatings and serious injuries on those who fell into his hands. And if Simmons failed to nab anyone in the community on whom he could discharge his wrath, that would usually just mean more tough luck for his wife and daughters.

On what turned out to be a fateful day in 1830, the tavern keeper announced to his family he needed to go to Detroit. His wife, fearing he would use the occasion to drink, accompanied Simmons in hopes of keeping him out of saloons. She was successful until the trip home, when he stopped at the Black Horse Tavern for a few drinks. When they finally arrived home, Mrs. Simmons, exhausted from the journey, went straight to bed while her husband stabled the horses.

It's not known if Mrs. Simmons was asleep when her husband entered their bedroom with a gallon jug of whiskey. If so, she was soon awakened. After taking several long swigs from the jug, Simmons demanded his wife join him in a drink. She took a small sip hoping to mollify the man and keep his rage corked. By this time, the two daughters, hoping to escape their father's temper, had fled to their second-floor bedroom. When his wife refused to take another pull at the jug, Simmons exploded. He reared back and hit his wife in the stomach as hard as he could, driving the breath from her lungs. The woman gave a couple of breathless gasps but could not draw air.

When the sight of his wife lying on the bed as still as death penetrated his alcoholic rage, Simmons shouted for his two daughters to come and help. But their mother was beyond help and any further cruelty from her husband. Simmons was arrested for the killing and jailed in Detroit.

The low regard in which Simmons was held by the community became immediately apparent at the start of his trial. The court went through 138 prospective jurors before finding 12 who swore they could impartially judge the accused. Sober, well-dressed, and well-educated, Simmons hardly looked or acted like a killer — that is until the jury and the public heard the testimony. It was sensational stuff. C. Colton, who traveled throughout the Great Lakes in 1830 and recorded his observations in *Tour of the American Lakes* (1833), attended Simmons' sentencing. Shocked by what he heard, Colton wrote, "In the progress of the trial a history of savage violence was disclosed such, we would fain believe, as rarely passes upon the records of crimes." The author was further surprised to find that "the wretched man's own children were the principle witnesses on whose testimony he had been convicted."

To the surprise of many, the jury found Simmons guilty of murder, in spite of the fact it was clearly shown there was neither malice aforethought nor premeditation involved in Mrs. Simmons death.

Sentencing took place on July 26, 1830, and it was obvious to all that Simmons struggled to hold his emotions in check as he entered the courtroom. When asked if he had anything to say before the court pronounced sentencing, an unsteady Simmons rose and in a voice that broke with sobs replied, "Nothing, if it please the court." The judge then sentenced Stephen G. Simmons to death by hanging. Wayne County Sheriff Thomas S. Knapp thought the sentence unfair and declared he would resign rather than carry it out, whereupon Detroit hotelkeeper Benjamin Woolworth immediately stepped forward and said he wouldn't have any trouble putting a noose around Simmons' neck. When Territorial Governor Lewis Cass heard of Knapp's reluctance and Woolworth's remarks, he appointed Woolworth acting sheriff, causing Knapp to resign.

The new sheriff had a bit of showman in him, and he turned the execution into a public spectacle. Woolworth had several rows of benches built around three sides of the gallows and allowed vendors to erect booths in the jail yard from which refreshments were sold. As a captain of the local militia, he also arranged for a military band to perform a two-hour concert preceding the execution.

The day before the hanging, all roads within 50 miles of Detroit felt the steady tramp of people heading to the big event. The city's hotels and inns quickly filled to capacity, restaurants did a brisk business, and some homeowners made easy money by opening their residences to overnight boarders.

On September 24, 1830, the makeshift grandstands filled to overflowing, as did rooftops and trees with views of the gallows. Behind the grandstand the crowd stood shoulder to shoulder several rows deep, and behind them men on horseback listened to the music and waited for the main event to unfold. The *Northwestern Journal* estimated 2,000 people jammed into the area, a count which if anywhere near accurate meant one out of every 15 people residing in the territory were present at Sheriff Woolworth's extravaganza. One newspaper editor who studied the crowd wrote that he was pleased to see so many women at the event and even approved of the presence of mothers with young children.

At the conclusion of the band concert the jail door opened and Sheriff Woolworth and the condemned man walked arm-in-arm to the gallows. Simmons' face was pale, but he was otherwise composed, mounting the gallows' 13 steps without hesitation and then sitting in a chair. After the reading of his death warrant, Simmons rose and delivered a short but powerful speech on the evils of alcohol, confessed to the sorry events that had led to his present circumstances, and concluded with a plea for mercy from the territorial government. Then to the delight and surprise of the assemblage, in a rich baritone he sang a popular hymn of the period,

"Show pity, Lord, O Lord, forgive,
Let a repenting rebel live;
Are not Thy mercies full and free?
May not a sinner trust in Thee?

"My crimes are great, but can't surpass
The power and glory of Thy grace,
Great God, Thy nature hath no bound,
So let Thy pardoning love be found."

One witness later recalled that "Simmons sang (the) hymn in a voice in proportion to his size."

The condemned man's humble contrition and the beautifully sung hymn took some of the enthusiasm out of the party atmosphere. And if God might forgive and pardon, the territorial government couldn't or wouldn't. The sheriff positioned the condemned man over the trapdoor, placed the noose — made from stout rope in consideration of Simmons' weight — over his head, adjusted it so the knot lay just behind the left ear, and placed a cloth sack over his head. Woolworth then quickly stepped to the side and pulled the lever that dropped Simmons into eternity.

The execution left a bad taste in the mouths of many, including eye-witness L.D. Watson who years later wrote, "I witnessed the hanging and being quite young at the time the impression it left on my mind led me to think such punishment both cruel and vindictive." Simmons had faced his demise with dignity, but not much of the same could be found in any other aspect of the affair, and the festive atmosphere became a civic embarrassment. Public sentiment against capital punishment grew, and the backlash from Simmons' execution — the last in the Michigan Territory — even brought about the removal of Detroit's public whipping post from the corner of Jefferson and Woodward Avenues. Adding fuel to the anti-capital-punishment movement, in 1838 just across the Detroit River from Detroit, the Province of Ontario executed a man, then learned he was innocent.

Lawmakers and citizens did not forget that incident or what happened on September 24, 1830. On March 1, 1847, when the only 10-year-old State of Michigan issued a Revised Code, the penalty for murder was limited to imprisonment at hard labor for life. Michigan had become the first state in the Union — and, some researchers say, the first government in the English-speaking world — to abolish the death penalty.

Stephen Simmons' execution took place at the corner of Gratiot Avenue and Farmer Street, just three blocks south of Grand Circus Park. If the People Mover doesn't pass directly over the site of the gallows, it is certainly only a stones throw from the monorail tracks to it.

JAMES SOMMERS

The Michigan Homesteader's War

At first glance, this is a story that could have come straight out of a dime western novel. On one side stood homesteaders, who poured sweat, money, and hopes for a better life into land they could call their own. Opposing them were powerful business interests, including a lumber company with political connections and an army of lawyers. The bigshots — claiming the homesteaders were illegal squatters who owned neither the property nor the timber on it — ordered the cutting of trees on the disputed land.

But hey, the homesteaders weren't about to grab the "Monkey" Ward catalog, tip over the two-holer, and simply fade into the woods. But how to fight back? As if on cue, a loner named Jim Sommers turned up at a homesteaders' meeting and grabbed everyone's attention by suggesting ways to literally stop the lumber company in its tracks. Better yet, the stranger was a crack shot with a Winchester and quickly demonstrated his willingness to employ the rifle in their defense. Could this be a real life Shane? In the western U.P. the man did, in fact, become an outsized hero, a Lone Ranger who took up the cause of people treated unfairly by the law and the powerful.

In reality, however, Jim Sommers was a vicious sleazebag who'd been run out of half the towns in the U.P. He even had the singular distinction of somehow managing to limbo under the bar of Seney's incredibly low community standards and got the bum's rush out of that Helltown, U.S.A. As Jim picked himself up and dusted off his derriere, the ejection committee from Michigan's most notorious town ordered him to never come back. So he moved on to run a string of brothels in lumber towns throughout the U.P., while also gaining renown for his murderous temper.

In 1881 near Fayetteville on the Garden Peninsula, for instance, Sommers ran a little slice of sin called the Hole in the Ground. The picturesque little company town barred brothels or saloons within the city limits. But those of its citizens who wanted to raise some hell didn't have to go far, because several shady entrepreneurs, including Sommers, had set up brothels and saloons just a short walk from town. Area lumberjacks, sailors, and the town's men provided a steady clientele for all the dives.

Given the nature of Sommers' business, the townspeople were understandably surprised when, one day, a proper young woman from Milwaukee stepped off a passenger boat and walked to the nearest business, where she asked directions to Sommers' place. She said she had answered an ad in a paper offering employment as a companion for Sommers' invalid wife. The young woman quickly became the whispered talk of the town, because Jim didn't have a wife.

A few days later a freight train had hardly made it out of town when the crew spotted the beaten, bloodied, and probably deflowered Milwaukee woman lying beside the track. The crew helped her on board, took her back to town, and booked her a room in the Shelton Hotel. Word quickly spread of the young woman's fate, and townspeople then watched in stunned disbelief as Sommers drove a buckboard up to the hotel, grabbed the girl, and headed back to the Hole in the Ground.

The disbelief quickly turned to outrage, and as the sun dipped into Big Bay de Noc, an armed and angry band of men went after Sommers. The mob surrounded the Hole in the Ground, dragged Jim outside, beat him like a drum, and left him for dead on the bay shore. The gang then ransacked the bordello and found $2,000. They gave half the cash to the Milwaukee woman and divided the balance among the house prostitutes, who were then told find employment somewhere other than the Garden Peninsula. And finally before returning to town, the gang reduced the bordello to charred embers.

Sommers survived the beating and turned up in Manistique, where once again he wore out his welcome. The town found that Jim couldn't any more avoid crime than a moth could deny the attraction of light. The culmination of his brief stay in the area was summarized by the The Crystal Falls *Diamond Drill,* which reported Sommers had been "... at one time engaged in a nefarious trade in Schoolcraft County, near Manistique from which he was compelled to 'fly' having pounded one of his victims, a man named Jack Ham, nearly to death." If indeed Jim did "fly," it was because he became airborne when he was thrown out of the county.

He landed in Keweenaw County as the "Lone Ranger" ready and willing to fight for downtrodden homesteaders.

At its essence, the Homesteaders War was a land dispute over thousands of acres of prime timberland along the Paint River watershed in Iron County. The parcels were awarded by the federal government to the Portage Lake Ship Canal Company as payment for constructing the Portage Canal — a 2-mile long ditch connecting Lake Superior to Keweenaw Bay via Portage Lake and Portage River — which allows boats to pass through the middle of the Keweenaw Peninsula rather than around its tip. To turn their property payment into dollars, the Canal Company planned to harvest the valuable timber from the lands.

However, for reasons researchers have never been able to fully clarify, in virtually the last minute of his presidency, Grover Cleveland signed the 1889 Michigan Land Forfeiture Bill, which returned all of the canal company's land to the federal government and potentially opened it to homesteading. The company's Washington lawyers, of course, filed legal challenges, but in the western U.P., no one waited for clarification. Real Estate agents began selling the disputed land, and homesteaders threw up cabins and outhouses. Most staked out prime pine-covered lands, with some of the "homesteaders" actually being speculators who never intended to improve or live on their claims, but rather simply cut timber and make a quick, easy dollar.

But neither speculators nor honest homesteaders stood to profit when, in 1888, the Metropolitan Lumber Company either purchased from or contracted with the Canal Company the rights to harvest and mill timber from the vast Iron County acreage. In 1890 the company began construction of two sawmills and a company town named Atkinson on the north bank of the Paint River just below the confluence of the North and South branches of the river — an area that is remote even by U.P. standards. The company also established several lumber camps upriver.

And when the Metropolitan Lumber Company began cutting trees on the disputed land, they found they had a war on their hands.

The reasons for Sommers enlisting on the side of the homesteaders are not clear. Some say he was among those who had filed claims for disputed lands; others suggest speculators employed him to look after their interests. Another story has Sommers angry with the Metropolitan Lumber Company because of the firm's breach of backwoods etiquette. When a traveling lumberjack showed up in a lumber camp it was common practice to give the traveler a bed for the night and make a place for him in the cook tent. But when Jim showed up one evening at a Metropolitan Lumber Company camp, the welcome mat was pulled out from under him and he and his empty stomach were asked to leave.

Whatever Sommers' motivation, when the homesteaders first met and vowed to stop Metropolitan from lumbering their land, he emerged as a leader. Not only did he suggest the idea of halting logging operations by shooting the draft horses that pulled logs out of the woods, he also set the example the next morning by dropping the first team of horses to emerge from the forest. Soon, snipers lurked behind every other tree in Iron County, gunning down horses.

The carefully constructed ice roads over which logs were hauled on sleighs were also sabotaged, usually by women spreading hot ashes over them. And the actions of one, a Mrs. Patterson, make a good barometer of the level of desperation felt by some of the homesteaders. When Mrs. Patterson ran out of ashes, she laid down on an ice road to stop a loaded sleigh from reaching the mill.

Nevertheless, the company vowed to continue cutting trees and asked the sheriff for help. When a deputy arrived, however, he immediately realized the insurrection was too widespread to stop and left.

The conflict escalated. The company's livery equipment was stolen or destroyed, their sleighs burned, and the woods booby-trapped. When one company timber cruiser tripped the wire of a gun trap, the bullet passed between his knees, close enough to the family jewels to temporarily devalue them by several carats due to involuntary shrinkage. In the sawmills, water was let out of boilers, belts were cut, and gears jammed with scrap metal. Some of the logs that did reach the mill were as deadly as claymore mines. Saboteurs would drive spikes into the timber, and steel band-saw blades that hit them were turned into instant shrapnel that flew throughout the cutting room. Luckily, no serious injuries were ever reported.

The violence was neither one-sided nor nonlethal. One homesteader who tried to file on land the lumber company thought was rightfully theirs, was discovered dead, face down in a 3-inch-deep mud puddle. Locals claimed the man was murdered; the coroner announced death was from drowning.

Dedicated, bona fide homesteaders also fought battles on the legal front. They planned to farm their land but counted heavily on proceeds from the timber on it to buy farming equipment and livestock. So they hired lawyers to represent them in Washington and counter the battery of expensive attorneys retained by the lumber and canal companies. But the homesteaders' attorneys took their clients' money, lived the high life, and never pressed the case. Headway wasn't made on the homesteaders' behalf until 1895, when a small group of would-be landowners traveled to Washington and personally pled their case before President Grover Cleveland.

Sommers may have become a hero by shooting horses, but his participation in the Homesteader War ended in December 1891 when he shot a man. Ironically, the attempted murder had nothing to do with the land conflict and everything to do with Jim's pure cussedness. There are several versions of the incident; please pick your favorite.

The first version has Sommers entering Kate Harrington's saloon, which sat across the river from the Metropolitan Lumber Company's sawmills. A character named Jerry Mahoney had taken up residence in the saloon earlier and was hard at work looking for the bottom of a whiskey bottle. Mahoney was known to have a quick tongue attached to a brain that was dysfunctional when it came to self-preservation. Seeing Sommers, Jerry began taunting him about shooting horses and his past problems with the law. Jim warned Jerry to shut up or "he'd operate on Mahoney's tongue with his rifle" or words to that effect. The threat didn't slow Jerry's mouth down, and so after listening to further abuse, Jim left the saloon, crossed the street to a hotel, picked up his rifle, returned to the saloon, stuck the rifle through a gap in the siding, took careful aim, and shot Mahoney in the right cheek. The bullet passed through Mahoney's mouth, removed several teeth, carried away part of his tongue, and widened his smile.

Another version has Sommers entering the Harrington saloon and running into motor-mouth Mahoney. Mahoney saw an easy target for his trash talk and aimed several verbal jibes at Sommers, who finished his drink, picked up his Winchester, and said to Mahoney, "Fare de well canary" before shooting him under the ear with the same effect as the first version.

The first two versions were reportedly from eyewitnesses, but each story was told and retold and changed with every telling. The final variation on the story comes from the Crystal Falls *Diamond Drill*. The paper reported that Sommers entered Harrington's in a foul mood and badly in need of a drink, but not the means to acquire one. Jim asked Ross, the bartender, for the loan of a ten spot. Assessing the credit risk but not the risk to life and limb, the barkeep said no. Sommers said he'd be going then and asked for his rifle, which was behind the bar. Ross handed it over, and as the *Diamond Drill* reported, "No sooner had Sommers gained possession of the gun than he began to shoot carelessly around the room." One bullet chewed up the floor between Ross' feet, the second came within inches of nailing a customer at the bar, and the third missile slammed into Jerry Mahoney who had slept through the entire fracas. The bullet struck Mahoney in the face, near his ear and cut off part of his tongue." The *Diamond Drill* added that Sommers "... simply did the shooting in a fit of hideousness — one of his spasmodic characteristics." This version sounds credible, but it's hard to believe Mahoney slept through rifle fire coming from the same room in which he napped. Perhaps the paper was being kind, and the man with the sharp tongue had passed out.

Witnesses to the shooting carried Mahoney across the river to a first-aid clinic at the sawmill, where as the *Diamond Drill* speculated, "(his) chances of recovery are anything but flattering." Frontier medicine amounted to shaving the stubble off Mahoney's lacerated face and then sewing him up. The person wielding the needle and thread stitched what remained of Mahoney's tongue to the inside of his cheek, and when the wound became infected, the patient was taken to Iron River for some proper doctoring.

Surprisingly, the loss of part of his tongue didn't handicap Mahoney in the least. Regretfully some would say, he talked as good as ever, and although the wounding slowed him down for a while, he quickly returned to being a mouthy pain-in-the-ass. And again, sometime after the shooting when he was fully recovered, Mahoney's run-on mouth far outdistanced his instinct for self-preservation. He was having a hell of a good time verbally lacerating a slow-witted fellow when the guy finally snapped and began pounding Mahoney like he was Monday morning laundry. After knocking him down for the umpteenth time, the man asked Mahoney, "Do you want some more?" Mahoney replied, "No, I ain't no hog."

When news of the Mahoney shooting reached Sheriff Tully in Iron River, he headed for Harrington's on the Paint River, but Sommers was long gone. He had hung around the saloon for the rest of the day of the shooting, while the homesteaders passed a hat and gave the money to their hero. Then the next day, the rifleman slipped into the woods and disappeared.

Tully, upon returning to Iron River, posted a $100 reward for the gunman. The *L'Anse Sentinel* reported that "Jim Sommers, the Iron River man who shot Jerry Mahoney and all but killed him, is in the Upper Peninsula, but evades the officers. He carries a Winchester rifle and a brace of revolvers and officers are not anxious to approach him in the open field."

The *Diamond Drill* took umbrage with the L'Anse paper and replied, "Right there is where you are mistaken, Br'er Kinney. If, when you say officers, you include Sheriff Tully, the *Diamond Drill* must inform you that that gentleman is in no mood to be bluffed by Jim Sommers and that if he (the sheriff) meets the outlaw it will probably be a case of the survival of the quickest man, that is if Sommers has the courage to 'play at an even game,' which we doubt very much."

But Sheriff Tully never caught up with Sommers, and we'll never know who was the quickest man. Sommers simply disappeared never to be seen again.

The homesteaders' conflict with the Metropolitan Lumber Company dragged on for another four years, finally ending in 1896 when legitimate homesteaders, not speculators, were allowed by the federal government to keep their land and make improvements. But after all the years of weary struggle, many simply sold their timber rights to the lumber company at bargain-basement prices, and some even went to work for their old enemy.

DANNY DUNN

Duke of Hell

D anny Dunn was on the road to Hell long before he had any idea the route would take him to the U.P., where for a time he would be the most celebrated resident in a lawless village that gained national fame as "Helltown U.S.A."

The young Irish lumberjack — with red hair, quick-silver temper, and a mean streak a rabid wolverine would envy — first made a mark for himself in the lumber towns of the Saginaw Valley in the 1870s. There, in the midst of the state's lumber boom, Dunn spent more time looking for trouble than honest work. He may not have been much of a lumberjack, but he soon won a modest reputation as a brawler. The young tough was always ready for a fight, in spite of possessing neither great pugilistic skills nor size.

During fights in the woods north of Saginaw, size did count, but boxing technique was far less important than an unabashed willingness to win at whatever cost to fair play. Mike Tyson would have been considered a piker for only nibbling on Evander Holyfield's ear. In the pinery, entire ears and even noses were taken off by gnashing teeth. And sticking a thumb into an opponent's eye and then popping the ball clear of orbital bones was not considered out of the bounds of propriety.

Dunn not only embraced those brutal tactics, he also had an innate talent for making a weapon out of damn near anything close at hand — a bottle, chair, cue stick — and using it with damaging effect. But his greatest gift was the ability to judge when he was within moments of being reduced to chopped steak at the hands of a better fighter, discovering an avenue of escape, and running like hell.

Dunn's first brush with both fame and near disaster occurred in the early 1870s in a little nugget of violence called Camp 16. The rough-hewn timber town (later to be optimistically renamed Edenville) crouched on the shores of the Tittabawassee River some 20 miles upriver from Midland. Dunn happened to wander into a saloon where Silver Jack Driscoll, one of the greatest fighters to knock down a man in Michigan's north woods, was downing requisite in-training booze. Whether having drunk too much "squirrel whiskey" — a rotgut liquor lumberjacks claimed made them frisky enough to scamper up and down an oak and look for acorns — or from a streak of sheer, self-destructive bravado, the outclassed Dunn challenged Driscoll to a fight. Within seconds the undisputed heavyweight champion of tall timber turned Dunn's bravado into pain and wiped up the floor with the smaller man. Realizing he was in way over his head, Dunn pulled a knife. When Silver Jack momentarily drew back to reassess the situation, Dunn showed Olympic sprinter form as he raced through the door and disappeared into the night.

Not long after the Camp 16 fiasco, Dunn took a job bartending in a Roscommon saloon and bordello owned by John Mahoney. Given the chance to either fell trees with an ax or thirsty lumberjacks with bad whiskey, Danny quickly discovered the latter was not only easier but much more profitable. In early 1878 he opened his own bar and whorehouse near Roscommon and lured away many of his former employer's customers by offering the woman-starved lumberjacks better-looking prostitutes than those turning tricks at Mahoney's. "Dunn's Bull Pen," as he named his business, proved so successful he opened branch Bull Pens in nearby Prudenville and Houghton Lake plus a pool hall in East Tawas.

And it was in East Tawas where Dunn had his first and only serious run-in with the law. There on the Fourth of July, 1878, Danny and a shady sidekick named Jack Hayes spent the holiday drinking steadily in several saloons. With every bend of the elbow Dunn grew meaner, and as his blood alcohol count rose so did the certainty of a brawl.

Whether it started with a look or word, Danny got his fight, and in the whirlwind of fists, teeth, elbows, thumbs and feet, a gun (probably Dunn's) was drawn and shots fired. None of the brawl's many combatants were hit but, as the U.S. military likes to say, there was collateral damage. One of the slugs hit bystander Owen McDonald — who went by "Wee Ownie" — in the foot. As the reverberations of gunfire faded and hearing returned, Wee Ownie's strident cry, "I'm mortificating, I'm mortificating," filled the room.

When news of the brawl and shooting reached the law, Justice Hugh McDonald issued a warrant for Dunn's arrest, and Constable Bob Johnson and officer Davey were directed to bring him in. When the officers walked into the bar where Dunn had continued drinking, they encountered a hostile crowd fronted by a swaggering Jack Hayes, who brandished his gun and let the lawmen know he would not let Dunn be taken. Johnson and Davey withdrew to wait for a better opportunity, which was not long in coming.

Feeling immune from the law or being just too drunk to remember the law was after them, Dunn, Hayes, and a few fawning bar flies adjourned to the nearby American House saloon to continue their drinking. Johnson and Davey followed the raucous group into the bar and announced that Dunn was under arrest. Hayes immediately turned on Johnson, and as he battered the constable with his fists, Dunn jumped Davey. Dunn's cronies whooped and hollered in expectation of the lawmen receiving a sound beating, which looked like a certainty until Johnson suddenly palmed his sidearm and loosed three shots. The first flew wide of its mark, but the next two hit home, with one clipping Hayes' heart. He died while still swinging at Johnson. When Hayes fell and with gunshots still ringing in his ears, Dunn broke away from Davey, headed for a side door, and ran from the saloon. This time, however, Dunn didn't run fast or far enough. He was tracked down and arrested by nightfall.

Dunn stood trial for resisting arrest, the jury found him guilty, and the judge sentenced him to 18 months in Jackson State Prison. The community's grateful citizens hailed Constable Johnson as a hero and presented him with an engraved Smith & Wessen revolver, which is displayed at the Iosco County Museum.

By 1881 Dunn was out of jail and on hard times. Honest lawmen were making it difficult to earn a dishonest buck in some of Dunn's old haunts, and James Carr had opened a bordello in Harrison and had a strangle-hold on the beer and prostitution trade in Clare County. Never one to look kindly on competition, Carr tried various schemes to rid himself of Dunn. He hired drunks to complain to local authorities about Dunn's keeping a house of ill repute (which Carr was equally guilty of). When the charges didn't stick, Carr hired an arsonist to burn down a small-time competitor's saloon and then tried framing Dunn for the job. Carr had the law on his payroll, but the graft and corruption made the cops fat, lazy and ineffectual. As a result, Danny always managed to sniff out and side-step Carr's legal booby traps.

Fed up with the legal and illegal harassment, Dunn began searching for a better business climate for his stock and trade. Seney in the Upper Peninsula looked to be a perfect fit for a man with an itch for money and no qualms about how to make it. The town was plunked down alongside a logging railroad some 70 miles northwest of St. Ignace in a vast, flat plain covered with white pine. More often than not, each spring the area flooded, so most of the town's structures — wooden sidewalks, houses and saloons — were built on stilts three feet off the ground.

The town also quickly became a cesspool of sin and degradation. Several lumber camps stockpiled their logs on the banks of the nearby Fox River, and many lumberjacks found it unthinkable to return to camp without making the easy detour through Seney and sampling its whiskey and women.

So Dunn packed his personal belongings and headed for the U.P. enterprise zone, but not before paying an aging lackey $50 to put a match to his Roscommon bar. Some have speculated that Dunn had the bar burned for insurance money, but it's hard to imagine any insurance company writing a policy on a raw-boned whorehouse set down in Michigan's timberland. It seems more likely that the pinch-purse just wanted to make sure he left nothing behind anyone else could use.

Dunn hadn't been in Seney long, when the old man who'd torched the Roscommon bar showed up and demanded more money. It was a fatal miscalculation. Dunn lured the arsonist to an island in the nearby Fox River where he killed and buried him. When a druggist from the Lower Peninsula showed up a few months later and inquired as to when he would begin receiving payments on money he'd loaned Dunn, it was a prescription for death. Dunn led him to the same island and cancelled his debt. The bones of the two victims were discovered years later. Both bodies were dug up and reburied alongside countless other nameless men in the town's cemetery.

Dunn opened a saloon in town and a bordello on the outskirts and then contributed heavily to Seney's reigning reputation, during the decade of the 1880s, as the sin capital of Michigan. Some 20 saloons and two large whorehouses catered to the basest desires of lumberjacks, con men, crooks and drunks.

On days off, entire camps of loggers descended on the town for a day of barhopping. When one camp of loggers encountered a gang from another camp on Seney's streets, there would be a tense, wordless moment as the rivals sized each other up. Whatever the formula and however the body language was decoded, the two gangs either broke into smiles, jokes and backslapping, or within moments the gathering blossomed into a great free-for-all as the competing camps joyously attempted to beat each other senseless. Fighting came a close third to women and whiskey within the trinity of lumberjack entertainment, and it could get brutal. John Bellaire, a longtime resident of Seney remembered that the "Marquis of Queensbury would have found much to criticize as a witness to a typical fight."

Frank P. Bohn, Seney's first doctor, also left some memorable descriptions of the lawless town. Even though written in his old age, you can still sense the doctor's awe in recalling his early days there: "I have seen the streets and board sidewalks of the town literally swamped with fighting loggers. ... On my first Christmas there I worked all day and all night treating the fighters who could find their way to my office by following the red trail on the snow that reddened and broadened as the day wore on." On the first and many following Christmases, Doc observed, "The most marked and constant features of the day, and the nights before and after, indicated that brotherly love was absent and that peace on earth was gone and forgotten."

Dunn stocked his whorehouse with two-dozen women who reportedly were on par with the rest of Seney's prostitutes, which was not a ringing endorsement. Contemporaries complained that most of Seney's pros had been scraped from the bottom of a particularly nasty barrel. It wasn't just looks, but also comportment. Most of the working women chewed Peerless Tobacco. Now just a dribble of tobacco juice down a female's chin wouldn't necessarily take the bloom off the romance. But to see a woman turn her head while lying in bed and launch a highly viscous stream of brown liquid toward a distant spittoon did have the potential of wilting the ardor of the less-stout-hearted pleasure-seekers in those pre-Viagra days.

Also there were those women who wanted to dance before adjourning to the bedroom. "How nice," probably thought the customer, as he was waltzed around the floor, that is until his jaded lover steered him near a door where accomplices jumped the john, dragged him outside, stole his money, and left him hugging the cold, damp ground.

Regardless of looks and junkyard-dog seductiveness, the supply of Seney prostitutes often could not keep up with the demand. For Dunn and the Harcourt brothers, the other big whorehouse operators in Seney, it must have been like being given keys to the mint. The trade proved so good, even prostitutes bragged about making lots of money. One harlot was known to have saved several thousand dollars, and another boasted of having collected more than $1,500 just from lumberjacks' pants pockets while the men were in the throes of passion.

During the village's heyday, the demand for females became so great that a trainload of whores arrived in Seney every weekend. It's unknown whether these railroaded women were temps who suited up as "sporting girls" on weekends only or were fulltime pros from across the north country who rushed to Seney on weekends, like smelt dippers knowing all they had to do was dip their nets in the current. Whichever, the weekend reinforcements earned money — often in full and open view — in alleys, empty boxcars, and unoccupied buildings right up until the minute their train chugged out of town.

There is not an iota of exaggeration in Dr. Bohn's claim that "Seney acquired the reputation which made it possible for the pilgrim, who journeyed thither, to ask for a ticket to hell and be sure of being understood as wanting to go to Seney." Seney had become nationally infamous and commonly called "Helltown U.S.A."

As a result, a swarm of eastern reporters once descended on the area intent on uncovering even more sin and scandal. Gambling, whoring, and brawls they found at every turn, but that was old news. Then the journalists got their story. In reports trumpeted from coast to coast, they wrote electrifying, sensational articles about enslaved men forced to work in lumber camps. As evidence, the reporters described the Ram's Pasture, a building into which men were forced each night by armed guards and herded to the woods the next morning to cut timber.

The story, however, was sheer baloney fed to the gullible and over-eager newshounds by straight-faced lumberjacks who spent winters entertaining each other with other tall tales, many including Paul Bunyan. In truth the Ram's Pasture was a hotel where for 25-cents men could sleep off their drunks on the lobby floor. As a result, on weekends the lobby of the bargain lodging often became a wall-to-wall crazy quilt of snoring lumberjacks.

By the mid 1880s, Dunn, if not quite the king of Seney, at the least controlled a lucrative dukedom based on booze and prostitution. In fact, when Jim Carr, his old competitor from Clare County, came to town and offered to buy Dunn out for the then princely sum of $5,000, Danny laughed him out of his saloon. And it was not difficult to look on the Irishman as Helltown U.S.A.'s nobility. True, Dunn would just as soon kill, cheat, or rob you as look at you, but he personally didn't drink, gamble or swear. And unlike 99 percent of Seney's inhabitants, he always dressed impeccably and spoke softly. To the surprise of many, Dunn even met and married a very proper Victorian woman.

Danny became enough of a force in Schoolcraft County by 1888 that all he had to do was stand near polling booths to ensure Seney overwhelming voted for Dennis Heffron, his choice for county sheriff.

That same year Dunn also made a mockery of the judicial system. Charged with running a whorehouse, Dunn hired attorney Frank Peters of Newberry, who not only tied the prosecutor and his witnesses into verbal knots, but also made fools of those who testified. At times, the peels of laughter became so great the Manistique Circuit Court judge had to call for order. The defendant was found innocent because, under Peters' withering cross examination, no witness would swear Dunn operated a whorehouse.

The end of the trial found Dunn at the height of his power and wealth, but serious trouble and danger lay waiting just four doors north and across the street from his saloon.

Although some 20 saloons, two bordellos, and any number of freelance prostitutes operated in Seney, Dunn and six Harcourt brothers were indisputably the village's major purveyors of sin. The Harcourts, originally from Saginaw, had arrived in Seney before Dunn. Jim, the oldest, ran a bar on Main Street North, on the same block as Dunn's saloon, and also managed the town's other bordello. The other brothers held a variety of jobs at the bar and whorehouse. It must have galled the Harcourts to be first on the scene, then watch an upstart horn in on their business and become the unofficial crown prince of their little corner of Hell. Whether the simple result of unhealthy competition or instant visceral dislike, Dunn and the Harcourts feuded and the whole town knew it. Dr. Bohn recalled that their "rivalry was strong, bitter and extensive."

The feud came to a head on June 25, 1891, when Steve Harcourt, at 20 the youngest of the brothers, unaccountably decided to climb into the lion's cage and tweak the big cat's nose. One can only assume Steve was full of alcoholic bravado when he walked into Dunn's bar and ordered a drink plus a round for everybody in the place from Dunn himself. Dunn's Irish temper flared, and he refused to serve Steve. In turn, the youngest Harcourt verbally cataloged Dunn's shortcomings in life, including in all probability the art of love. The name-calling continued until one of the

Harcourt brothers saloon (rightmost building)

two punctuated their rebuttal with a whiskey bottle over their opponent's head. Eyewitnesses can't agree who swung the whiskey bottle, but it would seem the weapon would have been closer at hand for Dunn, who wouldn't have hesitated a second in using it.

There is only minor dispute as to what happened next. Steve pulled a gun and fired two shots at Dunn. The first struck Dunn in the hand and the second buried itself in the wall behind the bar. Before Harcourt could get off another round, Dunn grabbed a gun from under the bar and blasted a divot out of Steve's neck. As the youngest Harcourt recoiled from the wound, Dan put another bullet square in his breadbasket. Steve left a trail of blood across the saloon floor as he staggered outside before collapsing on the sidewalk. Friends helped him to his mother's house, where Dr. Bohn pronounced him "beyond help." Steve Harcourt died three days later and was laid to rest in Seney's cemetery.

Those in the bar at the start of the shootout raced from the saloon like they'd just heard news of an artesian well producing 80-proof Kentucky whiskey. Dunn closed the deserted bar, turned off the lights and, gun in hand, waited for the Harcourts. Finding himself still alive the next morning and the streets empty of his enemies, Dunn boarded a train for Manistique, where he turned himself in to Sheriff Heffron. A local judge and prosecuting attorney held a coroner's inquest, which found Dunn acted in self-defense. Downstate papers that covered the proceedings railed at the lawlessness of the U.P. and claimed Dunn paid off witnesses.

The remaining Harcourts were still grieving for their brother when they heard that Dunn had walked out of the inquest free of any charges. For the Harcourts, the news just supplied further proof that Dunn owned the sheriff, so the five brothers held their own inquest, which ended with them drawing straws to determine who would exact their form of justice. Jim picked the short straw and welcomed the chance to take revenge.

When Dunn returned to Seney, the second hand on his watch couldn't have made one revolution before he heard of the Harcourts' death threats. Dunn was so spooked by the news, he once more called upon his most trusted means of self-preservation. He and his wife fled Seney and took up temporary residence in St. Ignace. Dunn also contacted Judge Bowen of Manistique and had him issue a peace warrant against Jim Harcourt and two of his brothers. Sheriff Heffron was handed the unenviable task of serving the warrant and arresting the brothers. When Heffron arrived in Seney, the Harcourts simply refused to be arrested, but agreed to accompany the sheriff back to Manistique and talk with the judge.

For anyone going by rail to almost any place in the U.P. in the 1880s or '90s, travelers first had to take a train to Trout Lake, where they invariably waited for a connecting train heading to their destination. On July 26, 1891, the same day the Harcourts set off for Manistique with Sheriff Heffron, Dunn agreed to meet with his lawyer Frank Peters of Newberry at John Nevin's saloon in Trout Lake. When the Harcourts' train pulled into Trout Lake, the three brothers, along with the sheriff, stepped off the coach and headed to Nevin's for a drink while waiting for the Manistique-bound train.

Dunn was at the bar, with his back toward the door, talking with Peters when the Harcourts strode into the saloon. Jim Harcourt immediately recognized Dunn, quietly stepped up behind his brother's killer and, in the words of the *Sault Ste. Marie News*, "drew a self-acting 32-caliber revolver, held it within a foot of Dunn's back and fired three shots, with deadly effect, the victim expiring immediately." The first shot hit Dunn's left arm, the second clipped an artery near his heart, and third pulverized his spinal chord. Dunn died before he hit the floor, but Jim wasn't finished. He straddled Dunn and fired twice more at the victim's head, missing both times. Sheriff Heffron disarmed Jim after he'd emptied his five-shot revolver and took all of the brothers to Cline's Hotel to wait for a train bound for the Soo, where Heffron would hand Jim over to the Chippewa County Sheriff.

The *Sault Ste. Marie News* reported that, "Immediately after the victim was assassinated the three brothers laughed and exaltedly gloated over the dastardly deed. They went to a hotel, ate hearty suppers, and seemed greatly overjoyed. Sheriff Heffron said they were laughing and joking about the sad affair all the way to the Soo."

If the *Sault Ste. Marie News* was outraged over what they considered a "dastardly ... assassination," other papers viewed Dunn's murder as almost a public service. The *Iosco County Gazette*, for instance wrote, "It seems to be the general sentiment among those here who knew Dunn, that if his destroyer should be convicted of manslaughter and then immediately released on suspended sentence, it would be sufficiently severe."

Jim Harcourt claimed self-defense at his trial, and despite clear evidence he shot Dunn in the back, it took the jury seven votes to convict him. The judge sentenced Jim to 7½ years in Marquette State Prison, where he became a model prisoner. Meanwhile his wife circulated a petition claiming her husband had killed a ruthless criminal and instead of prison should receive a pension for life. After serving three years, Jim was pardoned by Governor John T. Rich. He returned to Seney, where he held public office and was later appointed conservation officer for Schoolcraft County, all of which seems to pretty near add up to a pension for life.

Within days of Dunn's death his saloon was torched, and though the fire attracted most of the townspeople, no one tried to douse the flames. As the crowd watched the place burn, someone shouted that they saw a chair rocking amid the smoke and fire and then added it could be nothing else than "Danny Dunn's soul rocking in hell."

Danny Dunn and the town he helped make famous died with him. Not long after Dunn's death the Alger Smith Lumber Company extended a rail line to Grand Marais, on Lake Superior. Seney's sawmill and company offices moved to the new town, and with much of the area lumbered out, camps also moved on. Seney's rough-and-tumble glory days became nothing more than memories. Today, sporting just couple of stores and a traffic light, Seney is little more than a small aneurysm on one of the U.P.'s main east/west arteries. Motorists on M-28, their eyes glazed by miles of swamp and a road that is ruler straight for miles, blow through Seney in less time than it took Jim Harcourt to back-shoot Danny Dunn.

BIBLIOGRAPHY

BOOKS

Arndt, Leslie E. *Bay County Story*. Detroit: Harlo Printing Co., 1982.

Barnes, Al. *Vinegar Tales & Other Tales of the Grand Traverse Region*. Detroit: Wayne State University Press., 1959.

Beck, Earl Clifton. *Lore of the Lumber Camps*. Ann Arbor: University of Michigan Press., 1948.

Beck, Earl Clifton. *Songs of the Michigan Lumberjacks*. Ann Arbor: University of Michigan Press., 1942.

Beck, Earl Clifton. *They Knew Paul Bunyan*. Ann Arbor: University of Michigan Press., 1956.

Berriman, Stan. *Upper Tittabawassee River Boom Towns*. 1970.

Catlin, George B. *The Story of Detroit*. Detroit: *Detroit News*., 1926.

Dodge, Roy L. *Ticket to Hell: A Saga of Michigan's Bad Men*. Roy L. Dodge., 1975.

Dorson, Richard. *Bloodstoppers & Bearwalkers*. Cambridge: Harvard University Press., 1980.

Doty, Sile. *The Life of Sile Doty 1800-1876*. Detroit: Alved., 1948.

Fitzmaurice, John W. *The Shanty Boy; or, Life in a Lumber Camp*. 1889.

Gross, Stuart. *Frankie and the Barons*. Fowlerville: Wilderness Adventure Books., 1991.

Hargreaves, Irene. *The Story of Logging the White Pine in the Saginaw Valley*. Bay City: Red Keg Press., 1964.

Holbrook, Stewart H. *Holy Old Mackinaw*. New York: MacMillan., 1956.

Jacques, Thomas Edward. *History of the Garden Peninsula*. Iron Mountain: Mid-Peninsula Library Cooperative., 1979.

Jamison, James K. *This Ontonagon Story*. Ontonagan: *Ontonagan Herald*., 1939.

Karamanski, Theodore. *Deep Woods Frontier*. Detroit: Wayne State University Press., 1989.

Kilar, Jeremy. *Michigan's Lumbertowns*. Detroit: Wayne State University Press., 1990.

Massie, Larry. *Voyages Into Michigan's Past*. Au Train: Avery Color Studios., 1988.

Meek, Forrest. *Michigan's Heartland 1900-1918*. Clare: Edgewood Press., 1979.

Meek, Forrest. *Michigan's Timber Battleground*. 1976.

Michigan Writer's Project. *Michigan: A Guide to the Wolverine State*. New York: Oxford., 1941.

Orr, Jack. *Lumberjacks & River Pearls: Memories of Manistique*. Manistique: *Pioneer-Tribune*., 1979.

Petersen, E.J. *North of Saginaw Bay*. Sand Lake: Tall Timber Press., 1953

Reimann, Lewis C. *Between the Iron & the Pine*. Ann Arbor: Edward Brothers., 1951.

Reimann, Lewis C. *Incredible Seney*. Ann Arbor: Northwoods Publisher., 1953.

Rogers City Centennial History. Rogers City: Rogers City Chamber of Commerce., 1971.

Thornton, Neil. *Law & Order North of Saginaw Bay*. Tawas: Printers Devil Press., 1988.

Wells, Robert W. *Daylight in the Swamp*. Garden City: Doubleday., 1978.

Wood, Ike. *One Hundred Years at Hard Labor: A History of Marquette State Prison*. KA-ED Publisher., 1985.

NEWSPAPERS

Bay City Times

Clare County Press

Clare Sentinel

Detroit Free Press

Detroit News

Diamond Drill (Crystal Falls)

Gladwin County Record

Grand Rapids Evening Press
Grand Rapids Herald
Harrison Cleaver and Standard
Iosco County New Herald Press
Iron Port (Escanaba)
Lake City Plain Dealer
L'Anse Sentinel
Marinette Eagle Star
Saginaw Courier Herald
Saginaw Morning Herald
Saginaw News
Sault Ste. Marie News

MAGAZINES
Michigan Alumnus Quarterly
Michigan History Magazine

THE AUTHOR

Tom Powers retired from the Flint Public Library in 1999 after 31 years of service in order to pursue writing, reading, traveling, laughter, watching hockey, and perfecting the art of enjoying life.

Powers' first book, *Natural Michigan*, was published in 1987, and the first edition of *Michigan State and National Parks: A Complete Guide* appeared in 1989. Revised editions of both books are still in print. His other

works include *Michigan in Quotes, Audubon Guide to National Wildlife Refuges*, and *Great Birding in the Great Lakes*, also all in print. The latter was published by Walloon Press, which Powers and his wife founded in 1997.

Powers also freelances, and his articles and other short pieces have appeared in several magazines.

Barbara, his wife of 38 years; their two children and their spouses; and five grandchildren bring constant joy to his life.